WOMEN IN SAUDI ARABIA TO

CW00498695

Also by Mona AlMunajjed

MEANING AND SIGNIFICANCE OF ARABIC NAMES FOR GIRLS
IN THE ARAB WORLD

Women in Saudi Arabia Today

Mona AlMunajjed

First published in Great Britain 1997 by
MACMILLAN PRESS LTD
Houndmills, Basingstoke, Hampshire RG21 6XS
and London
Companies and representatives
throughout the world

A catalogue record for this book is available
from the British Library.

ISBN 0–333–63812–3 hardcover
ISBN 0–333–65481–1 paperback

First published in the United States of America 1997 by
ST. MARTIN'S PRESS, INC.,
Scholarly and Reference Division,
175 Fifth Avenue,
New York, N.Y. 10010

ISBN 0–312–12988–2

Library of Congress Cataloging-in-Publication Data
AlMunajjed, Mona.
Women in Saudi Arabia today / Mona AlMunajjed.
p.   cm.
Includes bibliographical references and index.
ISBN 0–312–12988–2 (cloth)
1. Women—Saudi Arabia—Jeddah—Social conditions.   2. Women–
–Saudi Arabia—Jeddah—Economic conditions.   3. Women—Education–
–Saudi Arabia—Jeddah.   4. Women in development—Saudi Arabia–
–Jeddah.   5. Jeddah (Saudi Arabia)—Social conditions.   I. Title.
HQ1730.A65—1996
305.42'09538—dc20   95–31779
                                                                              CIP

© Mona AlMunajjed 1997

All rights reserved. No reproduction, copy or transmission of
this publication may be made without written permission.

No paragraph of this publication may be reproduced, copied or
transmitted save with written permission or in accordance with
the provisions of the Copyright, Designs and Patents Act 1988,
or under the terms of any licence permitting limited copying
issued by the Copyright Licensing Agency, 90 Tottenham Court
Road, London W1P 9HE.

Any person who does any unauthorised act in relation to this
publication may be liable to criminal prosecution and civil
claims for damages.

10   9   8   7   6   5   4   3   2   1
06   05   04   03   02   01   00   99   98   97

Printed and bound in Great Britain by
Antony Rowe Ltd, Chippenham, Wiltshire

Contents

Map of Saudi Arabia

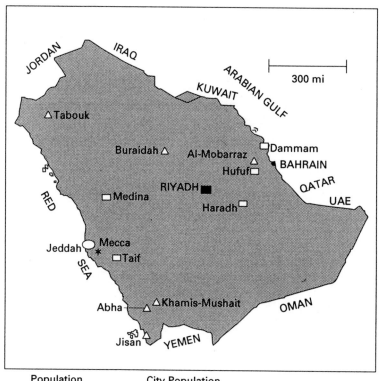

Population
16.9 million

Area (sq miles)
850,000

City Population

○ Over 1,000,000
* Over 500,000
□ Over 100,000
△ Under 100,000
■ Capital

1 Introduction: Saudi Arabia, Past and Present

Today, Saudi Arabia has become a major source of influence as the world's largest exporter of petroleum and oil products and is one of the richest countries in the world in its reserves of oil. Saudi Arabia is also the custodian of the two holy cities of Meccah and Medinah. It is in these cities that Islam was born at the end of the sixth century AD, developed under the Prophet Muhammad, and where the religion's holy book, the Qur'an, was revealed and written.

There are one billion Muslims in the world today, for whom the cities of Meccah and Medinah are holy places. It is to Meccah that hundreds of millions of Muslims turn to pray five times a day, and to where they come if they can, at least once in a lifetime, as pilgrims in obedience to their faith. All this has given Saudi Arabia a clear and leading status in the Islamic world. It has also led to the increase of Saudi Arabian participation in international relations concerned with Arab and Muslim countries.

Geographically, Saudi Arabia encompasses around 80 per cent of the Arabian Peninsula. It is bordered to the east by the Arabian Gulf, Bahrain, Qatar and the United Arab Emirates, to the south by the Yemen Republic and Oman, by the Red Sea to the west and by Jordan, Iraq and Kuwait to the north. The country occupies approximately 850,000 square miles. It is a land of highlands, plateaus and deserts. Most of the surface is covered by sand, forming the deserts of Nafud, Dahna and Rub al Khali (the 'Empty Quarter').

Saudi Arabia is divided into four major regions: Najd, Al Hijaz, Asir and Al Ahsa'. Administratively the country is divided into five major provinces. These are the Western Province (Al Hijaz), the Central Province (Najd), the Eastern Province (Al Ahsa', which contains the oil fields), the Southern Province (Asir) and the Northern Province (Tabouk). The major cities are Riyadh (the capital), Jeddah, Meccah, Medinah, Taif and Dammam.

The first and most important city is the Holy city of Meccah, spiritual capital of all Islam. It was the birthplace of the Prophet Muhammad (570 AD) and is the capital of Al Hijaz. Meccah includes the Ka'aba, built by Abraham and his son Isma'il. The Ka'aba is a stone structure and a site of worship for all Muslims.

Medinah, also situated in Al Hijaz, is the other Holy city of Islam. It shelters the tomb of the Prophet Muhammad in the green-domed mosque.

Riyadh, situated in the heart of central Najd, is the political and administrative capital city of Saudi Arabia. It was captured in 1902 by King Abdel Aziz, who used it as a base from which to reunify the Najd and most of the Arabian Peninsula.

Jeddah, located on the eastern shore of the Red Sea, has been for centuries the main port and commercial centre of Arabia. It was founded by Caliph Uthman ben Affan in 647 AD on the site of a fishing settlement. The original role of this city was that of port for the city of Meccah and a transit point for Eastern trade. Later it became the main importing and distribution centre for Al Hijaz, the western province. Today Jeddah is still the largest port on the Red Sea and it retains its traditional function as the pilgrim's gateway to Meccah.

Taif is the summer capital of the Hijaz. Dammam is the second largest cargo port after Jeddah. Located in the eastern region on the Arabian Gulf, it was constructed by ARAMCO (The Arab American Oil Company) following the discovery of oil. The city of Dammam serves as a commercial centre and is the main seaport for the Eastern and Central Provinces.

Saudi Arabia has a population of approximately 16.9 million (EIU, 1993/4). The majority of the inhabitants are Arabs of nomadic or semi-nomadic origin who, under the influence of rapid economic development, migrated to the major cities. Many of those who live in Najd or the central region are of pure Arab Bedouin origin and still maintain Bedouin traditions. The people of Al Hijaz in the western region are merchants by tradition and are of mixed racial origin. They are Muslims who came on pilgrimages from various countries (India, Indonesia, Turkey, Tunis, Yemen, Egypt, Syria) and settled in the major cities of Meccah, Medinah and Jeddah.

Saudi Arabia is a monarchy with a council of ministers. The political structure of the country is a unique blend of tribal custom and religious law and is headed by the Al Saud royal family. The country has strong roots in both religious and tribal history dating from the eighteenth century, when the first Ibn Saud (ruler of the town of Dariya in Najd) joined forces with a religious reformer, Muhammad ben Abdel Wahab, to form the political–religious Wahabi movement.

THE WAHABI MOVEMENT

In order to understand Saudi Arabia today it is necessary to study the Wahabi movement, which marked the start of modern Saudi Arabian history.

At the beginning of the eighteenth century Arabia was shut off from the outside world. Except for Meccah and Medinah, which were under Ottoman rule, it had degenerated into a state of ignorance and violence. The term 'Jahiliyya' (ignorance of the true religion) is used to describe this period, which was similar to Pre-Islam and was characterised by the corruption of norms and distortion of religious beliefs. The political situation was that of anarchy. Common legal rules and ties were nonexistent.

The Wahabi movement was a revivalistic movement organised by Muhammad ben Abdel Wahab and Muhammad ben Saud to revive what they perceived to be social virtues and to bring about a return to a former era of happiness: the 'Golden Age of Islam'. The Wahabis idealised the past, venerating the ideal picture of early Islam with its simplicity and strict orthodoxy. The period of Wahabiya started when a religious teacher from the Tamim tribe in Najd, Sheikh Muhammad ben Abdel Wahab (1703–92) (both his father and grandfather were Hanbali judges), began to preach for a return to the stern principles of Islam, stripped of all the innovations developed through the centuries, for example the excessive honouring of the Prophet and his companions. In combating syntheism, Abdel Wahab exalted the doctrine of Tawhid and the movement was better known as the 'Najdi Call' because it sought a religion of unity, as well as a need to purify the community by applying classical law – that is the Law of God – and returning to the ways of the Prophet and the first generations of pious Muslims, known as 'Al Salaf al Salih'. Wahabism also represents adherence to the letter of the Qur'an and the Hadith, which are considered the sole legitimate sources of authority, and adoption of the rigid interpretations of the Hanbali school, one of the most conservative of the four orthodox schools of Islam.

Muhammad ben Abdel Wahab's motivation to begin the movement was his extreme devotion to puritanical religion. The success of his movement depended on two important factors: faith and power. Persecuted in his home town of Ainiyya in Najd, Abdel Wahab found refuge with Emir (Prince) Muhammad ben Saud, the ruler of Dariya, who promptly became a convert. This conversion gave to Wahabism a political base upon which to build. An alliance took place between the emir and the sheikh to bring the Arab people back to what these men saw as the true faith of Islam.

Their alliance had a double purpose. In order to spread his teachings among the tribes and win converts, Abdel Wahab needed power and men, and these he found with the emir. For his part, Ibn Saud was ambitious. He was a leader and a soldier, and his motive for embracing Abdel Wahab's doctrine was more political than religious. By supporting Abdel Wahab's cause and extending the influence of Wahabiya he was able to establish control over the eastern and western Arabian territories. Both Muhammad ben Abdel Wahab and Muhammad ben Saud succeeded in fulfilling their aims, and the union of ideology and military force led to the birth of a state: Saudi Arabia. Leadership passed on to their descendants: Abdel Wahab's family, known as the Al El Sheikh, assumed the religious leadership of the country while the Al Saud descendants assumed political sovereignty.

After the death of Muhammad ben Saud in 1765 AD the political base of the movement weakened. The capturing of Meccah (which was under Ottoman rule) by Abdel Aziz ben Muhammad, the son of Ibn Saud, led the ruling Ottoman sultan to send in Egyptian forces to crush the Wahabi expansion in 1818.

It is important to note that throughout most of the modern history of the Arabian Peninsula a central political power was absent. The greater part of the country was a waterless desert that offered limited settlement opportunities to its nomadic population, who had no direct contact with the outside world.

Various tribes, who were in a constant state of warfare with each other, provided the basis for the social and political organisation of the peninsula. Power was exerted from the outside as the Ottomans controlled part of the peninsula (mainly Al Hijaz).

The Al Saud family's power was subdued by Muhammad Ali of Egypt in 1838, then by an alliance between the Ottomans and other northern tribes in the late nineteenth century. It was only in 1902 that they regained their power, when Abdel Aziz ben Saud returned from exile in Kuwait and captured Riyadh, thereby reestablishing the Al Saud dynasty. He was named by his father as Emir of Najd and Imam of Islam. Abdel Aziz fought against the Shammar tribes in the north and consolidated his power in central Arabia. Throughout his military campaigns Abdel Aziz spread forth the Wahabi religious reform, helped by the Ikhwan, a religious brotherhood of warriors. By 1926 he had captured the cities of Meccah, Medinah and the province of Hijaz. In 1932, after unifying the whole peninsula, Abdel Aziz declared himself King of Saudi Arabia.

Although the new kingdom was militarily and politically dominant in the peninsula, it was economically weak. The country's income came in the main from the exportation of goods such as dates, wool, horses and camels, but the most important source of income was the annual tax paid by pilgrims to Meccah.

In 1933 King Abdel Aziz granted an oil concession to the California Arabian Oil Company, a forerunner of ARAMCO, the Arabian American Oil Company. In 1938 oil was discovered in large commercial quantities and Saudi Arabia started to develop. The increase in the price of oil during the early 1970s, led to extremely rapid economic and material evolution, with the construction of schools, universities, houses and a very advanced communication system taking place in the 1970s and 1980s.

Although tribal and family loyalties remained strong, the advent of oil wealth weakened the influence of tribal authority. Demand for labour in the cities and for government posts led to a considerable number of people residing permanently outside their traditional areas. It also resulted in a massive influx of foreign workers to assist in the development of the country. Economic and industrial development continues, guided by the conviction that the long-term prosperity of the kingdom depends on investing oil income into more lasting forms of income-generating activities.

WHY A BOOK ON WOMEN IN SAUDI ARABIA?

The fact that Saudi women have become one of the most rapidly changing elements of society makes the issue of women in Saudi Arabia one of particular interest. Increasing concern with socio-economic development and the pressure to integrate women into the process of developmental change have become topics of extreme importance in the kingdom. The issue is subject to continuous debate. Saudi newspapers and magazines are full of articles arguing the pros and cons of a broader role for women in the social and economic life of the country. The literature is characterised by social and ideological schools that either favour or condemn the traditional role of women. Misconceptions about the status of Saudi women have distorted their true social image and depicted them as second-class citizens. It is true that traditional norms and cultural and patriarchal values have shaped the role of women in Saudi Arabia; however this should not be seen as an impediment to Saudi women taking part in the process of national development. The preservation of the traditional Saudi identity constitutes a natural and essential element in the evolution of the social entity of women in Saudi Arabia. Today Saudi women are contributing to and participating actively in the growth of the kingdom. Professional, educated women are eagerly seeking new opportunities in the labour market and are keen to play more responsible roles at the community level. Indeed, education and work outside the home have provided new horizons for Saudi women beyond the traditional confines of marriage and motherhood, and this has had a positive effect on their behaviour, self esteem, aspirations and relations with others.

This study attempts to examine and explore the quality of Saudi women's lives – that is, their social and subjective experiences in a traditional society – and to probe into the deeper meaning of their social reality. The Algerian writer Aisha Lemsine argues that 'we can understand the present Arabia only by questioning and probing the problems of its women' (Lemsine, 1983, p. 31). As a member of this society and sharing Saudi women's ideas, beliefs and personal experiences, I am able to understand the influence of cultural, traditional and patriarchal values on their status. In order to understand, therefore, the changing role of women in Saudi Arabia and the underlying social forces leading to these changes, I sought to understand the perception of gender roles as experienced by Saudi women. To this end I have used personal interviews, newspaper articles, data taken from religious, historical, sociological and anthropological studies (in Arabic, French and English) and my own knowledge of the subject.

DEVELOPMENT OF THE STUDY

Extensive interviews were conducted with 100 Saudi women in the city of Jeddah. These women share similar ethnic (Arab), religious (Muslim) and national (Saudi Arabian) social characteristics. They come from different geographical areas of Saudi Arabia (Jeddah, Meccah, Medinah, Gizan, Taif, Al Baha, Riyadh, Abha, the Eastern Province), belong to different Arab tribal groups (Al Asmar, Al Shamran, Madi, Al Ashkar) and represent different economic and educational levels. The units of analysis are two groups of women categorised according to level of education and employment:

1. A group of 50 educated women who are either in high school, have finished high school, are enrolled at the University of Jeddah or hold a University degree (BA, MA, or PhD). This group is divided into two subgroups: working and non-working.
2. A group of 50 uneducated women who are either illiterate or have attended elementary or intermediate school but stopped at one level or the other. This group too is divided into working and non-working.

I was not expecting to encounter difficulties in interviewing this large number of women. However I was mistaken because a researcher is not readily accepted in a traditional milieu that frowns upon those enquiring into other peoples' lives. A true random sample of women from each group was impossible to obtain due to difficulties such as a lack of pertinent information and statistics. I had to count initially on personal contacts – friends who trusted me enough to talk freely and answer my questions honestly. These friends introduced me to other women who were willing to cooperate because I was referred by people they trusted. It is not certain that the findings are typical of all Saudi women as they may reflect a bias inherent in the sample of women interviewed. Nevertheless the data is revealing of changes in attitude, and applies at the very least to a significant number of Saudi women. Under current circumstances this sort of sampling procedure is the best that can be hoped for, given the closed nature of Saudi society.

Interviewing Saudi women provided revealing information about their sentiments, opinions and attitudes regarding the essence and quality of their lives in a traditional society. They described their various experiences in education and work, which allowed identification of the most significant variables relating to the position of women in Saudi Arabia today. This constitutes the subject matter of the following chapters.

Chapters 1 and 2 provide an analytical account of major historical factors and religious processes that are essential to understanding the position of women in Saudi Arabia. Chapters 3 and 4 discuss the custom of segregation and veiling in Saudi Arabia which is described as a measure taken by society to protect the chastity of women and prevent other men from encroaching on the male honour of the family. At the same time it is a sign of respect and decency, and of identification with the traditional and nationalistic values of Saudi culture. Chapters 5 and 6 focus on the impact of education and paid employment on the status of women in Saudi Arabia. These chapters also study the resulting changes in women's attitude vis-à-vis their role in social and family life. Chapter 7 presents the conclusions of the study on women in Saudi Arabia.

2 The Status of Arab Women under Islamic Law

Saudi Arabia is an Islamic country that embraces the legal, economic and social precepts of Islam. Under Islamic law, men and women have basic legal rights in terms of marriage, property, divorce, inheritance, education and work. In Saudi Arabia today a woman cannot be forced to marry against her will; she has the right to choose whether or not to marry the person proposed to her. She even keeps her own maiden name after marriage. A Saudi woman also has rights of ownership and disposal of property and wealth before and after marriage. She may inherit from her father, husband, brother and son. She has the right to education, and the right to work in one of a number of occupations, as long as it does not affect negatively her family responsibilities.

In order to understand the social structure of the Saudi system in general, and more specifically the status of Saudi women, it is essential to study the direct relationship between Islamic thought and society. In Saudi Arabia, Islam acts as a major force in determining the institutional norms, patterns and structures of society. This is especially so since Islam is not only a religious ideology, but a whole comprehensive social system embracing detailed prescriptions for the entire way of life. In addition, the impact of Islam is a major factor affecting the traditional position, obligations and privileges of women in Saudi Arabia.

From its beginning Islam, which means the submission of one's will to that of God, has been a cultural and political entity as well as a religion. Its precepts provide guidance to Muslims in all social, political, commercial and economic affairs. The prescribed ways of acting are derived from two major sources: the Qur'an and the Hadith, or Sunnah.

The Qur'an is considered to be the complete revelation of God's message to the Prophet Muhammad. At the same time, for all Muslims it is a total spiritual, intellectual and behavioural guide to life.

The Hadith or Sunnah (traditions), is a collection of the sayings, teachings and interpretations of the Qur'an by the Prophet Muhammad and recorded by his closest companions, known as the 'Sahaba'. It also contains stories from the Prophet's life that serve as an example of moral and spiritual excellence that all Muslims are called upon to take as a model.

The Qur'an and the Sunnah are the basis of the Islamic Law or Shari'a (from the Arabic verb Sharaa, to legislate) which is characterised by its divine nature. In fact, in the Islamic concept, law precedes and moulds society. The other sources of the Shari'a are 'ijma'a' and 'quiyas'. Ijma'a consists of the consensus of learned scholars on particular problems whose solutions are not directly found in either the Qur'an or the Sunnah. They are solutions deduced from the Qur'an. Quiyas, which means measuring or comparing, stands for reasoning by analogy or interpretation. It permits the principles established by the Qur'an, Sunnah and ijma'a to be extended and applied to problems not covered by the other sources.

The basic immovable tenet of Islam is belief in the oneness of God and the prophecy of Muhammad. Along with it comes belief in all the preceding prophets, belief in angels and the day of judgement, praying five times a day, fasting during the month of Ramadan, paying an annual contribution 'zakat' for the poor and going on pilgrimage to Mecca at least once in a lifetime (the 'Five Pillars of Islam'). Other matters relating to daily life and worldly affairs are left to the interpretation of scholars who are well versed in the Qur'an and the Hadith. Therefore laws may vary with the passing of time only when these do not contradict the pillars of Islam.

The spirit and meaning of the Qur'an and the Sunnah have been variously interpreted by theological schools of jurisprudence in Sunni and Shi'a Islam. The four schools of Sunni Islam are the Hanafi, Maliki, Shafi'i and Hanbali. The most representative school of Shi'a Islam is the Jaa'fari school, attributed to Imam Jaa'far AlSadeq.

There are no fundamental differences between the orthodox schools as they all recognise the same principles of law, but they differ in their application. The Hanbali school conforms most closely to conservative orthodox thought. The theologian

Ahmad Ibn Hanbal, the master of Hanbalism, adhered strictly to the traditions of the Qur'an and his interpretation of them was literal. Unlike other imams he allowed a very narrow margin to the doctrines of ijma'a and quiyas. Saudi Arabia relies on Hanbali thought as its primary source of Islamic doctrine. Other Islamic countries, for example Kuwait and Bahrain, have adopted Shafi'i and Hanafi interpretations, which are known for their liberalism.

In order to understand the present position of women in Saudi Arabia it is necessary to evaluate the social position of Arab women during the early days of Islam. This chapter discusses the status of women under Islamic Law, and the rights and privileges that were accorded to them with the emergence of Islam in the Arabian Peninsula at the end of the sixth century AD.

What was the position of women before Islam? A brief historical account reveals their oppressed and powerless status in some of the ancient civilisations.

In ancient Greece, a woman was considered a creature below man and was deprived of civil rights. She was sold and purchased and had no right to inherit any kind of property. She was married without her prior consent and lived under the domination of a husband who could freely manage her money without interference from her (Afifi, 1932).

Under Roman law a woman was denied all judicial rights. She was subjected by reason of her sex to perpetual guardianship – by her father during childhood and by her husband for the rest of her life. She was an object to be possessed and inherited by men and had no right to inherit wealth or property from her husband (Al Dawalibi, 1981, pp. 15–16).

During the pre-Islamic period, which is known as Al Jahiliyya (the time of ignorance), women in Arabia lived in subjugation and degradation. The birth of a girl was looked upon as a disgrace and female infanticide was a widespread practice, especially among the Kindah, Rabi'a and Tamim tribes (Kahhala, 1983). The reasons for burying baby girls alive were to relieve parents from the economic burden they represented, and to relieve the tribe from any shame a girl could cause later by being caught as a prisoner during tribal feuds or falling into prostitu-

tion. Verses in the Qur'an condemning the practice of infanticide
declare:

> When news is brought to one of them, of
> [the birth of] a female [child], his face darkens,
> And he is filled with inward grief!
> With shame does he hide
> Himself from his people,
> Because of the bad news he has had!
>
> Shall he retain it
> On (sufferance and) contempt,
> Or bury it in the dust?
> Ah! What an evil (choice)
> They decide on?
>
> (Al Nahl, 16, verses 58, 59)
>
> When the female (infant)
> Buried alive, is questioned
>
> For what crime
> She was killed.
>
> (Al Takwir, 81, verses 8, 9)

At that time sexual permissiveness was the norm in Arabia, and
men had the right to an unlimited number of women. For example
a man could marry more than 10 wives at the same time (Karkar,
1979; Kahhala, 1984). Conversely, cases of polyandry existed,
where one woman was married to several men (*ziwaj al raht*). A
husband could have a mistress and the wife a lover without any
restrictions (*nikah al khazf*). Both husbands and wives could
exchange partners upon mutual agreement (*nikah al badal*).

Incest was practised, with fathers marrying their daughters. A
son was allowed to marry his stepmother after the death of his
father. Prostitutes were recognisable by a flag on their tents, and
men sought them whenever they liked (Al Bukhari, 1960,
p. 132; Kahhala, 1984, p. 13). A man could divorce his wife just
by saying the words of dismissal 'Go wherever you want', and
she had no redress to law. A woman was an object to be inherited

like money, but she could inherit nothing from her husband or her son.

With the emergence of Islam, female infanticide and sexual permissiveness were completely banned. Female infanticide became a crime against God, and the killing of a woman was considered a crime equal to that of killing a man. Islam sought to defend the rights of women and improve their standing. It decreased the marked differences that existed between men and women and recognized their independent status. The Qur'an lent support to basic equality between men and women by giving women equal rights with men (but not necessary identical), be they personal, civil, social or political rights. In the Qur'an, women are always mentioned along with men:

> And those who annoy
> Believing men and women
> Undeservedly, bear (on themselves)
> A calumny and a glaring sin.
> (Al Ahzab, 33, verse 58)

> Now, therefore, that
> There is no god
> But God, and ask
> Forgiveness for thy fault
> And for the men
> And women who believe
> For God knows how ye
> Move about and how
> Ye dwell in your homes.
> (Muhammad, 47, verse 19)

In another verse it is stated that men and women should be rewarded equally for proper conduct:

> Whoever works righteousness,
> Man or woman, and has Faith,
> Verily to him will we give
> A new life, a life
> That is good and pure, and we

> Will bestow on such their reward
> According to the best
> Of their actions.
>
> (Al Nahl, 16, verse 97)

The Qur'an specifies a number of virtues that are necessary to both men and women. Both sexes have spiritual as well as human rights and duties to an equal degree, and the 'future reward' of the hereafter is provided for the one as for the other:

> For Muslim men and women,
> For believing men and women,
> For devout men and women
> For true men and women
> For men and women who are
> Patient and constant, for men
> And women who humble themselves,
> For men and women who give
> In charity, for men and women who fast,
> For men and women who
> Guard their chastity, and
> For men and women who
> Engage much in God's remembrance
> For them has God prepared
> Forgiveness and great Reward.
>
> (Al Ahzab, 33, verse 35)

The Prophet himself made several statements concerning women, including 'He who honours women is honourable, he who insults them is lowly and mean' (Al Afghani, 1945, p. 55) and 'Treat your children equally. However, were I to favour some of them over others, I would favour the girls' (ibid., p. 58). In his last speech, given during the pilgrimage of farewell, the Prophet asserted that women should be taken care of: 'O People! Do take good care of women, you have rights over your women and they have rights over you' (Al Qannugi, 1976, p. 157).

Islam gave women equal rights with men to participate in social and religious activities, for example joining in prayers in the mosque and going to Meccah on pilgrimage (Rashid Rida, n.d., p. 11). During early Islam women in Meccah pledged allegiance to the Prophet (*mubaya'a*), vowing to worship no one but the one God, not to steal, not to indulge in sex outside marriage, not to commit infanticide, not to indulge in slander, and to obey the law and the principles of Islam. A verse in the Qur'an declares:

> O Prophet,
> When believing women come
> To thee to take the oath
> Of fealty to thee, that they
> Will not associate in worship
> Any other thing whatever
> With God, that they
> Will not steal, that they
> Will not commit adultery,
> That they will not kill their children
> That they will not utter
> Slander, intentionally forging
> Falsehood, and that they
> Will not disobey thee
> In any just matter,
> Then do thou receive
> Their fealty, and prey to God
> For the forgiveness: for God is
> Oft-Forgiving, Most Merciful.
> (Al Mumtahinah, 60, verse 12)

Both men and women are equally responsible for the welfare of the Muslim community and the maintenance of its spiritual and moral obligations by commanding what is right and forbidding what is wrong. As the Qur'an states:

> And the Believers, men
> And women, are protectors
> One of another: they enjoin
> What is just, and forbid
> What is evil: they observe
> Regular prayers, pay
> Zakat, and obey
> God and His Messenger.
> On them will God pour

His mercy: for God
Is Exalted in power, Wise.
(Al Tawbah, 9, verse 71)

In his Book, *Al Isabah fi Asmaa' Al Sahaba*, the fourteenth
century Arab historian Ibn Hajar mentioned that among the companions of the Prophet was a woman, Samraa' bint Nouhaik Al
Asadiyyah, who used to go around in the souks with a stick in
her hand, ordering the execution of good deeds while prohibiting
those that were wrong.

In another case, it was said that, after the death of the Prophet,
the Caliphate Omar ben el Khattab spoke at a Friday prayer gath-
ering and suggested that dowries be reduced to a symbolic sum
of not more than forty oukiya (1 oukiya = 250 grams), and that
any amount in excess of that sum should be given to the Beit al
Mal (House of Treasure). A woman rose at the back of the
mosque and objected, saying 'What is this Omar? God gave us
the right to keep our own dowry even if it were a "kintar" of
money' (1 kintar = 100 oukiya of gold, 1000 oukiya of silver or
4000 dinars (Ibn Manzour, 1970), and she quoted the following
verse from the Qur'an:

But if ye decide to take
One wife in place of another,
Even if ye had given the latter
A whole qintar (treasure) for dower
Take not the least bit of it back
Would ye take it by slander.
And a manifest sin?
(Al Nisaa', 4, verse 20)

The Caliphate immediately withdrew his suggestion, saying: 'A
woman is right, and Omar is wrong' (Al Qurtubi, 1967, p. 287).

Women were also granted the right to participate in political
affairs and to hold government positions. Aisha, one of the
Prophet's wives, took part in political events after the Prophet's
death and became a political leader in the fight against Ali ben Abi
Taleb in the 'Battle of the Camel'. Other women in Islamic history
became prominent political figures. For example Arwa bint Ahmad
Al Soulaihiyyah became Queen of Yemen after her husband fell ill.

She was described as a woman with a great personality, and she ruled Yemen for forty years until her death in 1137 AD. Safwat Al Mulk, a Seljuk woman who died in 1119 AD, became Queen of Damascus after deposing her son from the throne. Safiya Khatoun became Queen of Aleppo after the death of her son AlAziz and ruled 'with great justice and piety' before dying in 1242 AD. Finally, Shajarat Al Durr became Queen of Egypt after the death of her husband Najm Al Din Ayyub in 1249 AD. She led the battle against Saint Louis, the King of France, and was known for 'her extreme brightness and great intellect', (she was killed in 1257 AD) (Al Munajjed, Salahuddin, 1989).

In Islam, education and learning are revered and their importance stressed throughout the Qur'an. Islam made education and learning the equal duty of men and women. The first Qur'anic verse to be revealed to the Prophet Muhammad stated: 'Read, In the name of thy Lord ...' Who created ...,' (Al Alaq, 96, verse 1). Other verses mention the importance of education and knowledge, regardless of sex:

> ... God will raise up, to ranks
> (And degrees) those of you
> Who believe and who have
> Been granted knowledge. ...
> (Al Mujadalah, 58, verse 11)

> ... 'O my Lord! advance me
> In knowledge.'
> (Taha, 20, verse 114)

The Prophet declared that 'Seeking Education (Knowledge) is mandatory for every Muslim', both men and women. Other sayings from the Hadith in which the Prophet glorifies education regardless of sex are as follows 'The rank of Education is among the highest'; 'Scholars are the inheritors of the Prophets' (Musnad Ahmad); 'On the Day of Judgement, those who can intercede for Forgiveness are the Prophets, then the Scholars, then the Martyrs'; 'He who travels to seek Knowledge is struggling in the Path of God until his return'; and 'Seek Knowledge as far away as China'.

In a Hadith, related by Al Bukhari and Al Turmuzi, the Prophet also said: 'He who follows a Path seeking Knowledge follows a Path leading to Paradise, and the Angels bow humbly to the seeker of Knowledge in response to God's approval of him. Forgiveness is implored upon the scholar by all creatures on Earth and in the Heavens, even by the fish in the sea, and the distinction of the scholar is similar to the distinction of the full moon over the other planets'.

Islam proclaims that a woman cannot achieve perfection without acquiring knowledge. The Prophet himself asked Shaffa' bint Abdallah Al Qurashiyyah, an educated woman, to teach his wife, Hafsah bint Omar, to read and write (Rashid Rida, n.d., p. 17). A number of women asked the Prophet to accord them a day in which he would educate them about religious, ethical and moral matters, which he did.

Aisha, a wife of the Prophet, was well versed in medicine, Arab poetry and theology. After the Prophet's death she contributed with Umm Salamah (another wife of the Prophet) to the shaping of the early Islamic dogma. As they were considered the best first-hand authorities on the Prophet's life and teachings, they were consulted during the compiling of the Hadith, which along with the Qur'an forms the basis of the Shari'a. Aisha, who also acted as a judge and excelled in matters of education and literature, participated in the main political arena after the death of the Prophet.

Fatima Al Zahraa', daughter of the Prophet and wife of Ali ben Abi Taleb (the Prophet's cousin and the fourth caliph), was acclaimed as a very knowledgeable woman. She was prominent in poetry, history and theology. She gathered together all the companions of the Prophet (Al Sahaba) to give them lectures on ethical and moral codes (Al Abrashi, 1971, pp. 100–1; Kahhala, 1984, p. 108).

Soukainah bint Al Hussein ben Ali ben Abi Taleb (Seventh century AD), the daughter of Al Hussein, whose grandfather was the Prophet, was erudite in literature and poetry and her house was a meeting place for all the famous Arab poets, scholars and educated people (Al Abrashi, 1971, p. 101; Kahhala, 1984 p. 202). According to Ibn Abi Ousaibia' (died 1203 AD) in his book *Tabaquat Al Attibbaa'*, there were two famous women medical doctors during early Islam, one of whom was Zeinab, an expert on the treatment of eye diseases and a general surgeon for the tribe of bani Aoud (Al Abrashi, 1971, p. 106; Kahhala, 1984, p. 57).

According to the Qur'an and the Hadith, women are entitled to as much freedom of expression as men. In the early days of Islam women participated in serious discussions with the Prophet himself, as well as with other Muslim leaders. A verse in the Qur'an informs us how Khawla bint Tha'laba pleaded for help from the Prophet and God because her husband wanted to divorce her according to the old pagan custom of 'zihar', which freed the husband from all responsibility for conjugal duties but did not free the wife to leave her husband's home or to contract a second marriage. The verse says:

> God has indeed
> Heard (and accepted) the statement
> Of the woman who pleads
> With thee concerning her husband
> And carries her complaint
> (In prayer) to God:
> And God (always) hears
> The arguments between both
> Sides among you: for God
> Hears and sees (all things).
> (Al Mujadalah, 58, verse 1)

Her plea was accepted and the custom abolished.

Arab poetesses acted as community historians, journalists, social critics and political leaders (Aisha, for example). Among the most famous poets during the Prophet's time, was a woman named Al Khansaa', who started her career by reciting poetry at social events such as births, weddings and funerals. She also recited verses to arouse both men and women to fight for Islam. Her genius was her ability to improvise verses and she regularly won the highest prizes at the most prestigious poetry contest of the time, which was held annually for the general public at the fair of Ukaz, near Mecca.

The Qur'an gives all women the right to work and to earn money outside their homes, provided that this work does not result in harm to herself, her husband or her children. Muslim women have the right to work in commerce, industry and agriculture. The Qur'an declares: 'For men shall have of what they earn/And for women shall have of what they earn', (that is, individual property rights) (Al Nisaa', 4, verse 32). For example the wife of Abddallah ben abi Awfa carried stones during the construction of the Quibaa' mosque in Medinah (Kamel, 1980, p. 129).

Under Islam, women used to accompany Muslim armies and participate in battles. They nursed the wounded and prepared supplies for the warriors. Aisha and Umm Salim, among others, gave drinking water to the warriors during the battle of Uhud (Al Bukhari, 1960, p. 125).

Umm Atiyya Al Ansariyyah, a well-known expert in herbal medicine, joined the Prophet in seven battles as cook and nurse (Mouslem, 1928, p. 1447). Women also participated in wars and jihads (holy wars). A number of women warriors went into battle with the Prophet. Among them was Ammara Nusaiba bint Kaab al Mazinia, who joined the Prophet in the battle of Uhud and fought alongside her husband and sons in the Al Yamamah war after the death of the Prophet. It is said that she was proud to show off her battle scars, 'which were twelve' (Ibn Hisham, 1936, p. 320). The Prophet chose Roufaida Al Aslamiyya as the first Muslim woman to run a mobile hospital (a tent) for the wounded (Kahhala, 1984, p. 451).

Women in Islamic history have also contributed to welfare work. Zoubeida bint Jaafar, wife of the Caliph Haroun El Rashid (eighth century), saw to the transportation of water to pilgrims in Meccah from a place ten miles away. She also installed wells and tanks of water all along the pilgrim road from Baghdad to Meccah (Kahhala, 1984, p. 27).

During the Abbassid dynasty (749–1258 AD), women worked as secretaries to the caliphs and teachers of their children, instructing them in music, literature, Arabic calligraphy and poetry (Al Jahiz, 1979, pp. 156–7).

Islam grants women the right to own and dispose of their own property and wealth both before and after marriage, including the use of their 'mahr' or dowry given by the man to his bride.

A verse in the Qur'an states:

> [...] And it is not lawful for you,
> (Men), to take back
> Any of your gifts (from your wives)
> Except when both parties
> Fear that they would be
> Unable to keep the limits
> Ordained by God [...]
>
> (Al Baquara, 2, verse 229)

A husband has no right to any portion or share of his wife's property without her consent (Wafi, n.d., p. 14). Women are given equal rights to men with respect to entering into contracts, running enterprises and having independent earnings and possessions. They are free to mortgage their properties or to lease, bequeath, sell or otherwise exploit them for their own benefit (ibid, n.d., p. 7). Women can be economically independent and are not required to have intermediaries, trustees, or mediators.

Islam also gives women the right to inherit from their fathers, husbands, brothers and sons: A verse in the Qur'an declares:

> From what is left by parents
> And those nearest related
> There is a share for men
> And a share for women,
> Whether the property be small
> Or large, a determinate share.
>
> (Al Nisaa', 4, verse 7)

However women inherit only half the share of men because the Shari'a states that it is the duty of men to spend their money on women be this a father spending on his daughter, a husband on his wife or a brother on his sister. A woman is therefore entitled to the security provided by husband, father or brother (Rashid Rida, n.d., p. 21). This is interpreted as a sign of the honour and privilege that are bestowed on Muslim women.

As stated at the start of this chapter, Muslim women cannot be forced to marry against their will. Islam accords women the right to decide whether to marry and to approve, or not, their choice of a husband. The Prophet, according to Bukhari, said: 'He who marries his daughter against her will, has not concluded a valid marriage'. In another Hadith the Prophet said: 'No widow or divorcée is to be married without her consent, and no virgin without her assent, and her assent is her silence'.

In Islam, marriage is a contract, a civil act that is in accordance with religious precepts. The Shari'a does not prescribe any particular form of marriage ceremony as long as there are two witnesses. The payment of a 'mahr' or dowry to the bride is part of the contract. Islam has made it legally binding for a man to pay the woman he intends to marry a reasonable amount of money to safeguard her economic position after marriage. Regarding the size of a dowry, Islam has given a wide latitude to both men and women. It can be as low or as high as the parties desire. Usually the mahr is given in two parts: the first normally consists of jewellery given to the bride at the wedding; the second is usually a sum of money that is given in the event of divorce or upon the death of the husband.

It is stated in the Qur'an that marriage should be a union of love and tenderness, and that husbands should treat their wives with kindness and equity:

> And among His signs
> Is this, that He created
> For you mates from among
> Yourselves, that ye may
> Dwell in tranquillity with them,
> And He has put love
> And mercy between your (hearts)
> Verily in that are Signs
> For those who reflect.
>   (Al Roum, 30, verse 21)

> [...] And live with them
> On a footing of kindness and equity
> If ye take a dislike to them
> It may be that ye dislike
> A thing, and God brings about
> Through it a great deal of good.
>   (Al Nisaa', 4, verse 19)

In a Hadith the Prophet said: 'Let not any Muslim be harsh in his treatment of his wife; for if certain aspects of her conduct displease the husband, certain others will please him'. It is a fundamental tenet of Islam that a man has a duty to take care of the well-being of his wife and to provide her with lodging, clothing and nourishment. The Prophet said that 'the best Muslim is the one who is best to his wife, and that the greatest and most blessed joy in life is to have a good righteous wife'.

Muslim women keep their maiden names after marriage and may use those names when undertaking any sale or purchase transactions. Mothers are accorded high honour and recognition. Verses in the Qur'an declare that both parents should be honoured with kindness, respect and gratitude:

> We have enjoined on man
> Kindness to his parents:
> In pain did his mother
> Bear him, and in pain
> Did she give him birth.
> The carrying of the (child)
> To his weaning is
> (a period) of thirty months [...]
>   (Al Ahquaf 46, verse 15)

> Thy Lord hath decreed
> That ye worship none but Him,
> And that ye be kind to parents.
> Whether one or both of them attain
> Old age in thy life,
> Say not to them a word
> Of contempt, nor repel them,
> But address them
> In terms of honour
>   (Al Israa', 17, verse 23)

> And, out of kindness,
> Lower to them the wing
> Of humility, and say:

>   My Lord! bestow on them
>   Thy Mercy even as they
>   Cherished me in childhood.
>
>   (Al Israa', 17, verse 24)

In a Hadith, the Prophet said 'Paradise lies at the feet of mothers'. In another it is given to be understood that a mother is even preferred to the father. According to Abi Horairah (one of the Prophet's companions) a man came to see the Prophet and asked him to whom he should show the most concern and kindness. The Prophet replied 'Your mother'. Then the man asked who else? The Prophet again replied 'Your mother'. The man repeated the question and the reply was again 'Your mother'. The fourth time the man asked, the Prophet replied 'Your father' (Al Abrashi, 1971, p. 40).

Islam accords both men and women the right to divorce. Divorce was widespread before Islam among Arabs, Romans, and Greeks, and was permissible for Jews and Christians (the latter only in the event of adultery). However in a Hadith it is stated that 'The most hateful thing to God is divorce,' and Islam allows divorce only for specific causes of conflict between husband and wife, and as a preventive measure against adultery.

Polygamy was practised before Islam among the Romans, the Greeks, the Jews, the early Christians and the Arab tribes during Al Jahiliyya (Al Abrashi, 1971, pp. 63–65). Islam limited the maximum number of wives a man could have to four, then it decreed that a second, third or fourth marriage could not take place unless a man felt that he could do justice to all his wives, and could treat them with perfect equality in emotion, affection and material things. However, as this is difficult to fulfill, the recommendation is for monogamy. The relevant verse in the Qur'an declares:

>   And if ye fear that ye shall not
>   Be able to deal justly
>   With the orphans,
>   Marry women of your choice,
>   Two, or three, or four;
>   But if ye fear that ye shall not
>   Be able to deal justly (with them)

> Then only one, or
> That your right hands possess.
> That will be more suitable,
> To prevent you from doing injustice.
> (Al Nisaa', 4, verse 3)

In another verse:

> Ye are never able
> To do justice
> Between wives,
> Even if it is your ardent desire
> But turn not away
> (From a woman) altogether,
> So as to leave her (as it were)
> Hanging (in the air) [...]
> (Al Nisaa', 4, verse 129)

The practice of veiling (covering the face and seclusion) is not part of Islamic Law. The Prophet did advise women to cover themselves modestly, but not to cover their faces. The practices of veiling and seclusion were adopted by the Arabs from previous civilisations mainly by the upper classes as a sign of status and prestige (Levy, 1965; Hatem, 1985; El Khayat-Bennai, 1985; Lerner, 1986; Hashem, 1987).

Islam has been interpreted as presenting a kind of inequity in some of the Qur'anic injunctions concerning women. For example, a verse in the Qur'an declares: 'Men are "qawwamun" over women in matters where God gave some of them more than others, and in what they spend of their money' (Al Nisaa', 4, verse 34).

Several interpreters of the Qur'an have concluded that in Islam a woman holds a subordinate position. Some define the Arabic word 'qawwamun' as having a high standing, or being superior to someone. This interpretation is not without controversy. According to Al Qurtubi in *Al Jameh li Ahkam Al Qur'an* (1967, p. 168), 'qawwamun' means to be in charge of spending on women and protecting them, not 'superior to them'. A man is assigned the responsibility of leading the family and providing for its expenses. Men are favoured over women because (a) their physical constitution makes them more capable of taking responsibility for the whole family, and (b) the rules of inheritance allow a woman only half the share of a man. As mentioned, the rationale for this difference is that it is the man's duty to spend on the woman and provide her with food, clothing and lodging, as it is the man's duty to pay the 'Mahr' for the bride. Another verse from the Qur'an declares:

> And For Women Shall be
> Similar Rights in Fairness ·
> And men have a (darajah) Degree over them.
> > (Al Baquara, 2, verse 228)

This verse means that the sexes enjoy equality in law, but that the difference in nature and economic position between them makes men's rights and liabilities a little greater than women's (the Qur'an, Yusuf Ali translation, 1983, p. 90).

In *The Dictionary and Glossary of the Qur'an*, the word 'darajah' is defined as a step in rank, honour or authority (Penrice, n.d., p. 47). According to Al Tabari's interpretation *Tafsir Al Tabari* (n.d., p. 536), 'darajah' means rank or position. Al Qurtubi in his book, '*Al Jameh Li Ahkam Al Qur'an*' (1967, p. 124), explains the meaning of 'darajah' as 'manzilah' or position, and notes that men are given a higher position than women because of certain qualities they possess with regard to mind, strength, capability of spending, inheritance and engaging in 'jihad', as only men are required to participate in holy wars, not women. Ibn Abbas, uncle of the Prophet, said that use of the word 'darajah' implies putting pressure on men to behave with kindness and consideration towards women, and to be generous in spending money on them (Al Qurtubi, 1967, p. 125).

The Shari'a, including the Qur'an and the Hadith, are often seen as the main determinants of the status of Arab women. A debate over the position of women in Islam has dealt with the question of whether Islam sustains women's rights or undermines them. A review of the literature indicates that several trends have emerged in the Arab world, with some expressing more favourable views than others on the rights given to women in Islam.

Defenders of the position that women are equal to men in Islam maintain that Islam gives women equal civil and political rights with men in terms of seeking an education, inheritance, keeping their own names, conducting their own businesses and maintaining their own wealth. The Egyptian author Amina Al Saeed insists that Islam emancipated women as 'it came in terms of a greater social revolution in the history of all women's conditions' (Al Saeed, 1967, pp. 11–12:10). She argues that 'a woman during ancient civilizations had no rights whatsoever, and were not given any respect. But with the emergence of religion, the status of women considerably changed, as it provided them with all the rights of getting an education, selling, buying, working and participating in social and political affairs' (ibid., p. 11).

THE MUSLIM TRADITIONALISTS

Among the Muslim traditionalists who adhere to the above view are religious men such as Sheikh Hassan Al Banna (who was head of the Muslim Brotherhood in Egypt and was killed in 1949) and Sheikh Muhammad Mutawalli Sha'rawi, an Egyptian scholar. Both maintain that Islam had elevated the role of women and made them partners with men in terms of civil rights and social duties.

Al Banna considers that the relationship between a man and a woman should be built on the principle of cooperation between them and the ability to bear the difficulties of life (Al Banna, 1983, pp. 9–11). He encouraged the education of both men and women, and established a teaching centre in Al Ismailiyya (Egypt) to give young women a religious education (Kahhala 1983, p. 184).

Sha'rawi states that a woman's role as mother is more important than a man's role as father as it is she who has to raise the children and take care of them. Discussing the problem of equality between men and women, Sha'rawi wonders why people who demand the equality of women with men do not ask for the equality of men with women. He argues that 'these people are asking that a woman performs a man's job, however, they should require that the man performs at the same time the work and responsibilities of the woman, so that the principle of equality could be achieved' (Zein, 1987, p. 148). Sha'rawi adds that 'if a woman performs the man's job, and keeps also her basic responsibilities, then it means that they are putting a heavier burden on her' (ibid.)

Abbas Mahmud Al Akkad, one of the greatest writers of contemporary Arab history and the most conservative of Muslim traditionalists asserts that Islam has honoured women by lifting from them the curse of the eternal sin. However, Al Akkad rejects the principle of equality between men and women, and argues that due to biological differences men are superior to women (Al Akkad, n.d., p. 8). Therefore it is not within the realm of women to have social and political rights, but only those rights that pertain to being a mother, and a wife. Al Akkad claims that Islam has confirmed the natural differences between men and women and that God favours men over women (ibid., p. 7). He cites as evidence this verse in the Qur'an: 'And For Women Shall be Similar Rights in Fairness And Men Have a Degree over them' (Al Baquara 2, verse 228).

THE REFORMISTS

Other Islamic scholars, however, such as the Muslim reformists, consider that the 'backwardness' of Arab women in Islamic countries is not due to the teachings of Islam, but rather to misinterpretation of the Qur'anic verses and the adoption of extra-Islamic customs and traditions. According to the Islamic reformists the salvation of Arab women lies in their seeking emancipation within Islam itself, that is, by returning to the basic foundations and true principles of the Shari'a.

Most of the men who started the movement to reform the status of Arab women in the nineteenth and early twentieth centuries came from Egypt but followed the European tradition of reforms, a consequence no doubt of Arab countries being colonised by England and France. Among the first leaders during the colonial period were religious men in Egypt (which was a major cultural centre) such as Jamal al Din Al Afghani (1838–97) and Sheikh Muhammad Abduh (1849–1905). Both, with their progressive ideas, attempted to free Islam from the orthodoxy into which it had fallen and to pave the way for the emancipation of Arab women.

Al Afghani, who originally came from Afghanistan, stated that women are superior to men as they accomplish more in society by bringing up their children and raising a generation of men, teaching them the real ethics and morals of conduct (Amara, 1968, p. 529). Al Afghani was not opposed to the idea of women not being veiled, as long as the face was not used as a means to attract men for illicit conduct (ibid., p. 524).

Abduh criticised the inferior position accorded to Arab Muslim women and argued that Islam in its essence had assigned women to an equal position with men, and that this equality should be enforced in society. He added that 'the mind should be freed from the ties of tradition as one should understand the true meaning of religion by going back to its early sources' (Amara, 1980, p. 171). Abduh also called for the expansion of women's educational opportunities by not limiting their education to religious teachings only. He insisted that the weakening of Arab society was due to the ignorance of Arab women as a result of their being deprived of education relating to 'worldly affairs' (ibid., p. 27). Abduh stressed, therefore, that women's education was necessary to the evolution of the 'Ummah' (nation), and that it was the duty of all men to facilitate this by respecting women's rights. Abduh was attacked by conservative religious authorities and thinkers on different occasions, and much of his life was spent in exile outside Egypt.

Sheikh Rifa'a Rafii' El Tahtawi (1801–73) was another Egyptian religious man who called for the emancipation of Arab Muslim women. In his book *A Guide to the Education of the Girls and Boys* (1872), El Tahtawi insisted on the need to educate Arab women and to liberate them from the injustices of social traditions. He argued that 'God created the woman for the man so that each reaches his aim, and so that she would share with him his work. ... She is like him, exactly equal to him, they have similar natural characteristics to the extent that a woman could be considered a man ...' (Loutfy, 1985, p. 104).

The Muslim reformist Qassim Amin (1863–1908) transformed the cause of Arab Muslim women into a feminist movement. Amin, a lawyer, wrote two books on the subject of Arab women,

Tahrir al Maraa' (published in 1900) and *Al Maraa' al Jadida* (published in 1911). Like Sheikh Muhammad Abduh, Amin's call for the emancipation of Arab women did not imply a rejection of Islam, but only reform of the customs and social practices that had distorted the real image of Islam. Solutions to the problem of women should be found within the true framework of the Shari'a. In *Tahrir al Maraa'*, Amin argued: 'Yes, I come with an innovation, however it is not of the essence of Islam, rather it is of customs and methods of interaction in which it is good to seek perfection' (1970 edition, p. 31).

Amin called for the restitution of equality between the sexes and the liberation of women through education. According to him, the education of women would primarily benefit men as it would result in better mothers and better wives for the new generation of educated, Westernised Arab men (ibid., pp. 131–2). Amin also demanded the removal of the veil, the participation of women in all jobs and changes to some social practices, for example that they should be consulted in the choice of a future husband and that the practice of polygamy should only be allowed under certain circumstances. Although Qassim Amin drew exclusively on the teachings of Islam, he was severely attacked by religious authorities and conservative leaders for his liberal ideas, and for wanting to change women's role as mere wives and mothers of children. At the same time they rejected the norms of Western civilisation and objected to the removal of the veil as it could lead, according to their argument, to the public exposure of women.

Twenty years after the publication of Amin's first book on the emancipation of woman, Huda Sha'rawi (1882–1947), a pioneer and an activist for women's rights in Egypt, took off the veil in public. In 1910 Sha'rawi, a teacher, opened the first school for girls in Egypt to offer general education rather than vocational training. In 1920 she became head of the first Egyptian association for women (Fernea and Bazirgan, 1980, p. 119). She took part in demonstrations that took place in Cairo against the British occupation, and in 1923 she took the decisive step to remove her veil, which to her was a symbol of women's inferior status (Kaddy, 1980, pp. 146–7). Slowly other Egyptian women began to follow her example, and this voluntary removal of the veil marked the beginning of the gradual emancipation of Arab women.

In Lebanon, Nazirah Zein ed-Din was one of the first women to remove her veil. In 1928 she published a book entitled *Removing The Veil and Veiling*, which includes lectures and reflections on women's liberation and social reform in the Islamic world. Although the book was severely attacked by Muslim conservatives, it was highly acclaimed by Arabs all over the world, and by the Arab Academy in Damascus, Syria (Zein ed-din, 1982, pp. 221–6).

Also in Lebanon Sheikh Soubhi El Saleh, a religious Muslim reformer who was assassinated in 1984, insisted that Islam should honour women as girls and as mothers and that they should enjoy full legal and social rights. El Saleh argued that Islam established no differences between men and women (ibid., p. 10). According to him, 'a woman should not be seen as an object of pleasure for a man or only as a means for providing children' (El Saleh, 1980, p. 24). A woman, according to El Saleh, must be a man's partner in bringing up children and should share and participate with him in all matters of life. However El Saleh noted that the problem of Arab women lies in the discrepancy in applying the institutions of Islam, as men in most Muslim societies still underestimate the role played by women and do not look upon them with respect. Furthermore, women are still dominated by the family and feel that they are not wanted (ibid., p. 11). El Saleh explained that this feeling of rejection persists among women due to the disappearance of the real essence of Islam behind social traditions.

CONCLUSION

Controversy about the position of women in Islam persists in all Arab and foreign literature. In order to understand this conflict and resolve the controversy, more attention should be given to removing the preconceived notions about the status of women in Islam. This can be achieved by differentiating between the teachings of Islam as a religion and a way of life, and the local customs and social traditions that are not part of religion but which are often erroneously conceived as part of it. Religious documents are often unclear and are therefore subject to many different interpretations. Except for the basic immovable tenets of Islam (belief in the oneness of God and the prophecy of Muhammad) and the five pillars of the religion, matters that relate to daily life and behaviour are open to the interpretation of scholars of the various theological schools of jurisprudence.

This chapter has analysed the controversy over the role of women in the Islamic religion. In my view the preponderance of evidence shows that the Qur'an and the Prophet Muhammad's sayings did not set forth any doctrines or practices aimed at relegating women to an inferior or unequal position to men. On the contrary, there is an abundance of evidence in both the Qur'an and the Hadith to show that women are considered the equal of men with all the legal, political, economic and social rights of men.

In the development of gender roles in Islamic countries the role of women varies widely. Countries such as Bahrain, Kuwait, Tunisia, Egypt, Syria, Iraq, Jordan, Morocco, Yemen and Saudi Arabia differ significantly in the degree to which women have been emancipated from traditional social practices such as veiling, seclusion, educational opportunities and work independence. We must look, then, at the forces shaping the role of women in Saudi society in order to understand how these institutions and practices are affecting Saudi women in today's world.

3 Segregation

By law, women do not mix with unrelated men in Saudi Arabia. Sexual segregation is a general rule that touches on virtually every aspect of public and social life. Education, banking, access to public transportation and job opportunities are still rooted in strongly held traditional values that do not permit the mixing of the sexes. Almost all public places have areas that are restricted to women. Restaurants have special family dining rooms for women, and hospitals have separate waiting rooms for women. There are shopping centres exclusively for women, and certain boutiques in Jeddah have a closed door with 'For Ladies Only' written on it. Buses are divided into two sections to create a separate seating area for women. Banks have women-only branches. The zoo in Riyadh sets aside three days for women and three days for men.

According to Lipsky, 'there is a strong sense in Arabian society of what is public and what is private. Women (in Saudi Arabia), belong to the private world' (Lipsky, 1959, p. 298). In this segregated world the male–female dichotomy is linked to a public–private world where females are associated with the concept of indoors and males with outdoors. Deaver (1980) describes the social segregation between the sexes in Saudi Arabia and notes that:

> Public space is male space. It is the area of business and political activity. Mosques are also in the public domain. Thus, economic, political and religious activity are associated with the male. Private space is associated with females, kinsmen, gardens and intimate relationships. The private domain may be seen as a kind of retreat, a sanctuary .... Women ... belong to the private domain. To protect this sanctuary of the private space is the duty of all males. This is accomplished architecturally through externally opaque surfaces, tightly controlled access areas, and internal courtyards to provide outside space (Deaver, 1980, p. 32).

Houses in Jeddah, as in other parts of the kingdom, include a distinct area where women entertain each other away from men.

When women invite female friends for a social visit, they sit in a private section of the house, and male family members are informed ahead of time not to go into the room. Almost all weddings are segregated. They are considered a major social event and are meticulously planned weeks or months in advance. Weddings provide Saudi women with an opportunity to look at each other, talk about each other and display their beauty, their gold, their silk dresses.

The practice of segregation and confining women to their own company is an institutional mechanism designed to regulate women. Restrictions placed on women's mobility reflect the particular importance given by society to the concept of 'family honour', as the honour of a woman's father, husband and brother is tied to her sexual conduct. In an Arab Islamic society such as Saudi Arabia, a woman is committing a sin if she indulges in illicit sexual behaviour known as 'zina', which includes sexual intercourse between a man and a woman not married to each other. It applies to adultery and to fornication, which in its strict sense implies that both parties are unmarried.

Both adultery and premarital sex are therefore considered 'haram', that is, taboo and forbidden. Islam demands sexual purity for both men and women before marriage, sexual fidelity during marriage and abstinence after the dissolution of marriage. Those guilty of illicit practices are considered to be committing a 'dhanb', a grave sin. Verses in the Qur'an indicate this:

> Nor come nigh to adultery:
> For it is shameful deed
> And an evil way.
> (Al Israa', 17, verse 32)

Although both men and women are required not to indulge in illicit sexual relations, it is only the conduct of a woman – her chastity and fidelity – that is considered of vital importance for the pride and honour of the family. This is why precautions such as segregation and seclusion are taken by the male members to safeguard the purity of their women from any illicit conduct.

According to Patai, the roots of the concept of male honour 'go deep into the structure and dynamics of the Arab kin group', tied by blood and patrilineal descent. He argues that even if a woman marries into a different kin group, she 'never ceases to be a member of her own paternal family. Her paternal family, in turn, continues to be responsible for her' (1983, p. 119). The honour of the family that is connected to the chastity of women and has a sacred character is called 'Ird'. Dodd (1973), defines the concept of 'Ird' as a controlling value that legitimates the family structure and a modesty code for both men and women. He notes that 'Ird' is associated with the virtue and reputation of women, and is evident in tribal, peasant and contemporary urban sectors of Arab society. Dodd summarises the pattern of 'Ird' as follows:

1. Ird appears to be a secular value rather than a religious one. The term does not appear in the Qur'an, although both the term and the very high value attached to it existed among the pre-islamic Arabs. Islamic teachings regarding women's status and male-female relationships may be regarded as supporting Ird indirectly, but it is not per se an Islamic pattern ...

2. Ird is an attribute both of individuals and of a group. A man has Ird, but it is in large part a reflection of the Ird of his family and his lineage ...

3. Enforcement of norms defending Ird is carried out primarily by the agnates: father, brother, father's brothers and agnatic cousins. These men are the possessors of the Ird ...

4. Once lost, Ird is difficult to regain. It can be lost through a single act in a brief space of time, and may take generations to restore ...

5. ... The Ird of a family can be raised or lowered, depending on the demeanor of its women (and the conduct of men towards its women) ...

6. The penalties for violation of the norms surrounding Ird are severe and may include death. These are the penalties inflicted by men on women of their own family ...

9. ... Ird is a matter of reputation even more than of fact ...

10. Ird is primarily a possession of the males, but the women of the family may come to take responsibility for the

observance and enforcement of the code ... (Dodd, 1973, pp. 40–54).

Dodd concludes that although certain forces of change such as urbanisation, social revolution and education may weaken the value of Ird, this value and its associated norms still resist the processes of change.

Arab sensitivity to Ird has resulted in the whole of Saudi society being structured in such a way as to keep 'a woman within strictly defined limits that make it difficult if not impossible for her to lose her sexual virtue' (Mackay, 1987, p. 124). Separation of the sexes is therefore maintained physically, socially and psychologically. Sex is psychologically and socially processed into gender. A system of rules, mores and beliefs deemed to be appropriate to each sex are expressed in the values, customs and laws pertaining to the education and working systems of the country. Jessie Bernard (1987), commenting on the separate worlds of men and women, argues that:

> as a result of these physical, psychological, and social processes, a host of cultural prescriptions and expectations arise which constitute a reality of incalculable power to guide, shape and control – that is to 'genderize' – behavior. So taken for granted are the walls of the world that surround each individual, that they are rarely noticed and even more rarely breached. Once such a separating two-world pattern of work and space allocation has been established, it tends to perpetuate itself (Bernard, 1987, pp. 26–7).

In Saudi Arabia the elaborate system of sexual segregation starts at school. Girls and boys are separated at the age of six and a series of duplicate schools are necessary in all towns. Girls and women students may be taught only by women teachers, so in most colleges and universities the problem of a shortage of women teachers is overcome by use of a closed circuit television, so that a male lecturer can teach the women and answer their questions by phone – they can see him, but he cannot see them. Indeed segregation is a deeply ingrained social custom in the country and the principle of coeducation is widely rejected. In answer to my question, 'Should young men and women attend together the same classes and schools at all levels?' 60 per cent of both educated and non-educated women interviewed disapproved of coeducation. 'I refuse coeducation', one of them replied. 'A child has to understand from his early years that it is not decent for a man to mix with women, even if it is in the field of education' (a 21 year old high school graduate, married).

The socialisation processes of six year old boys and girls are designed to set clear definitions of male and female qualities. Sexual differentiation is therefore reproduced in the school system for the social organisation of gender.

A 22 year old single woman (elementary level) said that she rejected the system of coeducation, because 'our social traditions do not allow that women mix freely with men, even in schools'. 'It is all a question of custom, attitude, habit and practice' explained a 19 year old single woman who works as a janitor in one of the welfare associations in Jeddah. 'If we were accustomed to attending classes with men since our childhood, then things would have been very different by now ' ...

A 28 year old single woman who holds a BA in business administration and works in a bank in Jeddah, said: 'Our cultural milieu does not approve of coeducation. ... As a matter of fact, it is much easier to be without men at school as otherwise it will be more difficult for girls to concentrate on their studies and they will spend all their time taking care of their physical appearance ... You see, there are too many complications when men are around'.

Segregation for most of these women is not only a way of life, it has become a safeguard against 'too many complications' arising in the presence of men.

A 36 year old illiterate from Jizan, married with seven daughters and two sons, said: 'Even if my daughter wears the Hijab, I will never allow her to go to school with boys. ... Remember, the honour of a girl is the most important thing and it is a must to protect it'. 'I do not approve of coeducation' another woman insisted, taking as an example the immorality of the Western world. 'A lot of problems may happen in schools, especially among teenagers and adolescents ... Look at all the problems of teenage abortions they are having in the United States ... Do you call that education?' (28 year old, BA, married, three children).

A number of contradicting arguments were raised by the 40 per cent of women who approved of coeducation. They clearly stated that coeducation 'develops self-confidence in a woman, and teaches her how to deal with men'. A young woman explained that 'it is very important to blend with men so as to know and learn about their mentalities ... and maybe we can even manage to change it' (21 year old BA, married, two daughters).

A 35 year old woman with an MA in education thought that 'the existence of men among us women, should be something very natural'. Another woman shared that view and added 'I have no objections to a mixed school system. I was myself in a mixed school in Cairo. A child should be raised in a non-segregated system' (42 year old, BA, divorced, two children).

A young teacher at the University of King Abdel Aziz in Jeddah stated her opinion on the matter: 'Although our school policy does not include men, I would eventually encourage a mixed staff of professors; this would give us a lot of gains in terms of exchange of information, especially as there are more Saudi men holding a PhD degree than women, and so it will upgrade us'.

A 46 year old woman with a BA in teaching and working in one of the women's welfare societies in Jeddah argued: 'I do not have any problem with studying with men ... as long as I know how to behave in terms of brotherhood and friendship. ... I am a respectable woman, and they have to respect me'. Another added: 'I think that it is irrelevant whether there are men or not in a class. ... It all depends on the way a woman behaves and the extent to which she can control her own behaviour with absolute decency' (35 year old with a BA in home economics, married, four children, owns her own hairdressing salon).

Most of the women who approved of coeducation expressed concern about the cultural problem in Saudi society, indicating that 'although we do not object to the principle, it is still too early to talk about coeducation in Saudi Arabia as tribal and cultural values are still very strong'. As a woman with a PhD in sociology put it: 'Don't forget that we are dealing with the values and the local traditions of a whole culture ... and it takes years and years, one generation after another to change the mentality and behaviour of people. ... Girls and boys are not socialised from childhood to study together or to mix with each other. ... It is seen as something shameful that must never happen'.

A 29 year old with an MA in social work and teaching in a school in Jeddah expressed the same view, adding: 'I don't mind the thought of coeducation, but local traditions are still strong. ... Our society is not yet ready for the idea of boys and girls growing up together and going to school together. ... Our values and traditions are important for the preservation of our identity as Saudi Arabians, but at the same time we need to accept the wave of progress and modernisation so that we can compete with the West, intellectually and economically'.

In Saudi Arabia, the elaborate system of sexual segregation found in the educational system applies also to the world of work, where women are confined to exclusive fields where there is no physical contact with men. Women are restricted to the domestic domain of 'female' work such as teaching, nursing and so on.

'Would you like to work in a non-segregated system?', I asked the women interviewees. Sixty per cent of educated and non-educated women said they would refuse to work with men. The main reasons given by most women for their refusal to work in close proximity with men were fairly similar to those given by the opponents of coeducation, with customs and local traditions being cited as significant factors. A 35 year old married woman with a BA in home economics and working in a sportswear boutique exclusively for women said: 'I would not work with men. ... Our society does not accept that ... and I could never get used to the idea of mixing with them.' A 23 year old illiterate with five children also thought that 'it is not decent or proper to mix with men as it is not the custom in our society'. For these women, mixing with men was considered a violation of the norms established by society, a lack of respect for proper ethical conduct as it could lead to illicit sexual behaviour.

While some women found that tradition prevents women from working with men, others argued that Islam is the real reason for the sexual segregation of women in economic and public life. A 27 year old high school graduate who was married with four children, explained that 'it is contradictory to our Shari'a [Islamic law] to mix with men ... Islam does not allow the mixing of the sexes for fear of temptation and adultery ... even if a woman has no bad intentions, the Proverb says: "the Devil is an Expert ... "' However, an illiterate 38 year old, mother of four disagreed, saying: 'Everywhere we go, they remind us "the Golden Rule for every woman is never to mingle with men" in order to prevent us from having problems with men ... But frankly, Islam is tolerant and whoever wants problems gets them, regardless of whether you are in the presence of men or not'.

Neither the Qur'an nor the Hadith, indicate that women should be prevented from participating in public life, although Islam does warn against the mixing of men and women lest it lead to seduction and the 'evil consequences' that might follow. The Shari'a prohibits contact between unrelated men and women. A woman should be accompanied by her father, husband or brother (Mahram) and she may not stay in privacy with a man unless she has her Mahram with her'. In Saudi Arabia it is officially deemed that women have no right to mix or socialise with unrelated men.

The Qur'an does not specify whether women should be completely separated from the sphere of men. Verses in the Qur'an declare:

> O Consorts of the Prophet
> Ye are not like any
> Of the (other) women [...]
>   (Al Ahzab 33, verse 32)

> And stay in your
> Homes and do not display your finery
> as women used to do in the former days of
> ignorance (jahiliyya).
>   (Al Ahzab, 33, verse 33)

This verse was addressed only to the Prophet's wives, in that they had to remain in their houses. The object was not to restrict their liberty, but to distinguish them from other women and to protect them from harm and molestation. Even Abbas Mahmud Al Akkad (died 1964), the most conservative of Muslim writers, argued that this verse was directed at the Prophet's wives on a specific occasion, and not at all women. Also, interpretations of the word 'quarna' (stay) may differ. According to the Great Islamic scholar Al Qurtubi (died in 1272 AD) 'quarna' may come from the verb 'waquara' or 'wiquar', which means respect, that is, have dignity and serenity in your homes (Al Qurtubi, 1967, pp. 178–9). The meaning could also be regarded as 'Quirna', which comes from the verb 'Quarara', to remain at home. Thus, there is no command in the Qur'an that states that all women should stay in seclusion at home. However the conservative interpretation of this verse has led to the argument that if the wives of the Prophet were told to stay at home, then it also implies that all women should do the same.

Islamic history indicates that the segregation of women was unknown to Arabs during the Prophet's days. Arabs then lived as nomadic tribes who never cloistered their women. It was only when the Arab conquerors established themselves in the big cities that segregation emerged as a way of life. During early Islam women participated in social and political life side by side with men. Khadija, the first wife of the Prophet, ran her own caravan business in Meccah, and she advised and financed the Prophet in his struggle to found Islam.

Women were also allowed to pray with men. In fact the Prophet appointed Umm Waraquah, a learned woman and one of the best students of the Qur'an, to act as imam in leading the prayers of the men and women of her large household. Under Islam, women were entitled to as much freedom of expression as men; they participated in serious discussions with the Prophet himself, as well as with other Muslim leaders.

Several reports in the Hadith describe women's visibility and participation in communal patterns. Men and women frequently met in the streets and greeted each other. 'In the homes, there was social contact, between the sexes, so that men and women knew each other personally, even if they were not closely related. ... There are also reports on women acting as hostesses to the husband's guests' (Stowasser, 1984, p. 36). As discussed in Chapter 2, Muslim women had the right to participate in wars and jihads (holy wars), and a considerable number of women warriors fought along side the Prophet. Among them was Ammara Nusaiba Bint Ka'ab al Mazinia, who joined the Prophet in the battle of Uhud, and participated in fighting alongside with her husband and sons. She was proud to show off her battle scars (Hadith Nabawi). Others have acted as nurses for the wounded during the battles. Aisha, the Prophet's wife and his favourite, fought in several battles, after the Prophet's death, and was actively involved in political, cultural, and literary activities. Al Zuheir, a prominent scholar noted: 'I have not seen anyone who is more knowledgeable in theology, medicine, and poetry than Aisha' (Afifi 1921, 2:139).

All these examples prove that segregation of the sexes did not originate with Islam. Ghita El Khayat-Bennai (1985) argues that 'the segregation of women as a group, or the Harem, is not a privilege of the Arab or Muslim Civilization, but existed previously and was adapted according to the ethology proper to the Arabs and the Muslims. In Ancient China (2nd BC), as indicated in the Siao-hio, a girl was secluded from the age of ten. The area where girls got their education was in a closed inner court separated from the house where the men lived (El Khayat-Bennai, 1985, p. 30). In India, women were formerly secluded all their lives and were prisoners of the 'zenana' i.e. harem. Around 2 BC in ancient Greece, women and young girls spent their time in the 'gynoecium' or 'gynaeceum', which was a private apartment reserved for the women of their house. A gynaeceum had its own courtyard and inner garden. Virtuous women never left their apartments, and only ordinary people went out (ibid, p. 31). The gynaeceum was also a feature of Byzantine life: 'In the early church, there was a tradition of separate accommodation for men and women' (Waddy, 1980, p. 123), although Ottoman sultans in the fifteenth century 'did not segregate their wives, nor did they employ eunuchs to guard their women. ... It was from the Byzantines that these customs were passed on to the Turks' (ibid., p. 124).

The segregation of women emerged only later in Arab Muslim society, when Arab tribes started to settle in urban centres. Levy argues that the practice of secluding women was fully established approximately 150 years after the death of the Prophet. He adds that it was 'among the richer classes that women were shut off from the rest of the household under the charge of eunuchs' (Levy, 1965, pp. 91–134). With the increase in the number of slaves and concubines, seclusion and segregation became widespread among the upper and middle classes, as was the case among the Memluks in Egypt during the eighteenth and nineteenth centuries. The seclusion of Arab women therefore became an expression of wealth, feudality and male control over women. Kandiyoti describes the system of male supremacy as a characteristic of the Muslim Middle East. According to her, it is among the wealthier strata that 'the withdrawal of women from nondomestic work is frequently a mark of status institutionalized in various practices such as the Purdah system, and veiling' (Kandiyoti, 1988, p. 280). Describing the status of women in Morocco, Mernissi (1983) argues that a number of women feel that seclusion is a matter of pride and not a source of oppression as Westerners believe. She goes on to say that a harem, a 'supreme example of segregation, is considered most prestigious as it necessitates ... a financial investment for its maintenance (especially) when all services have to be provided at home'. Mernissi adds, 'women who are obliged to go out on the street for shopping or for work, are consequently submitted to a systematic harassing which is the result of the spatial separation between the sexes' (Mernissi, 1983, pp. 161–2).

Today in Saudi Arabia the seclusion of women is still an urban and not a tribal phenomenon practised among all classes and more specifically those of the wealthy upper and middle classes. As an expression of wealth, it is a sign that a man can afford servants to do the shopping and errands for the household.

Segregation also restricts women's activities outside the house. While the majority of the women interviewed said that they would not work with men because of customs or religious beliefs, others, both educated and non-educated, said that they could not work with men because male members of the family would prevent them from doing so. A 35 year old illiterate, married with five children, admitted: 'You know, my husband does not like the idea that I would be working in the company of men'. 'What if you work without his consent?' I asked. 'Never', she replied, 'Do you want him to divorce me?'

In a traditional patriarchal society it is the duty of a wife to respect and obey her husband. Most of the Western women who are married to Saudi men conform to the strict norms of segregation and veiling. As one American woman said: 'Why not? I live in this country, and I should abide by the customs'. Then she added: 'and my husband wants that'.

For a single 24 year old woman (Elementary level) it was family that prevented her from working. As she put it: 'My family would not agree at all ... especially my father, he would not accept my working with men. ... I have to accept that. He is my father, and you must know very well that it is "Ayb" [shameful] to say "No" to your father. He protects our honour ... and they taught me in school that the "Rida" [contentment] of Allah [God] comes from the Rida of your parents.'

In Saudi Arabia a child is expected to respect both parents, especially the father since he is the head of the household. In Islam parental authority is a respected norm and kindness to parents is considered an individual act of piety:

> Thy Lord hath decreed
> That ye worship none but Him,
> And that ye be kind To parents.
> Whether one or both of them attain
> Old age in thy life,
> Say not to them a word
> Of contempt, nor repel them,
> But address them
> In terms of honour.
> (Al Israa', 17, verse 23)

> And, out of kindness,
> Lower to them the wing
> Of humility, and say:
> My Lord, bestow on them
> Thy Mercy even as they
> Cherished me in childhood.
> (Al Israa', 17, verse 24)

Children are commanded to honour and cherish their father and mother with respect, kindness and humility. We cannot expect God's forgiveness if we are rude or unkind to those who brought us up. Thus Islam has reinforced traditional respect for parents.

By abiding by her father's wishes, a girl escapes his 'ghadab' (anger). Values regarding the ethical conduct of men and women support the religious norms of parental duty.

A large number of women rejected the idea of working with men for fear of male harassment. As an illiterate 30 year old married with eight children, said: 'Working with men would bring problems ... they would keep on harassing you, and pestering you all the time. I am sure they would even stop you from working'. An educated (BA level) woman of about the same age, married with four children and owner of a hairdressing salon, added: 'No ... I prefer not to work with men ... Anyway, men here do not take us seriously'.

Other women said that they would refuse to work with men for fear of being left alone with them. Whether educated or not, young or old, married or single, they all shared similar feelings of mistrust regarding men. As a single 23 years old with a BA in business put it: 'No, I would not work with men. ... It is just the idea of being with them that frightens me. ... They scare me, I don't trust them and I don't like to deal with them at all'. A 30 year old teacher with an MA in education commented: 'I am not against the idea of working with men. ... Unfortunately I feel that our men are not yet ready to mix with women'. A young PhD sociologist analysed the situation as follows:

> In our society there is no relationship of friendship between a man and a woman. A man will always be a male and there is no emotional maturity between a man and a woman ... they may fall in love with each other from the first time ... The fear is then how to interact with each other, and how to behave ... It is all a question of system, as the whole structure of our society is segregated. Segregation is not only in schools or work, but in everything else: weddings are segregated, hospitals are segregated (in certain areas), restaurants are segregated ... This is why the idea of mixing is very hard to accept, and it will require generations to change the traditional mentality.

Women who were willing to work with men were those who had studied abroad, lived for a while in a foreign country or frequently holidayed abroad with their parents; or those who would do so out of economic need, especially those from the lower income class.

A single woman of 42, who owns a clothing boutique where only women are allowed, acknowledged that she would very much like to work in a mixed environment: 'I even encourage it', she said, 'and I feel that if we are really living in the twentieth century, we cannot separate men from women. They complement each other ...' Another added: 'God created Adam and Eve. ... He did not separate them from each other. ... It is an essential part of natural law to have men and women mixing together. ... As long as each knows their limits, why not?' (32 year old BA married, two children, teacher).

Other women, both educated and non-educated, also liked the idea of women mixing with men, as long as they know how to behave in men's presence. As a 29 year old single woman with an MA in computer science put it: 'A man is just another human being, and work is work everywhere. ... As long as I am in a proper attire, wearing the Hijab, and knowing how to behave, then I do not think that there is anything to prevent me from working with men and playing a major role in helping my society'.

An illiterate 24 year old, married with five children and working as a janitor in one of the welfare associations, in Jeddah, gave voice to her feelings: 'There is nothing wrong with working with men. ... I don't accept the idea that a woman should sit at home and not work at all just because men might work in the same place. ... Especially if a woman needs to work to help her husband, like my husband who is 63 years old and is very sick. I don't care if men are around. ... Believe me, there is no shame, and nothing is shameful but the path of shame itself'. 'What if your husband says no?' 'Well we need the money, and there is no one to help us but Allah. ... Anyway my husband trusts me, and I know what is 'Haram' [in violation of religious laws] and what is 'Halal' [conforms to religious laws], my husband will not object'.

4 The Veil

The veil is the symbol of the seclusion of women. Boudhiba argues that Arab women's dress emerged as a result of the separation of the sexes. He explains that garments are an instrument of modesty and must 'hide the body, and at the same time reflect the sexual dichotomy of the world. This function (is) assumed from the female side by the (use of) the veil; (it) has a value which goes beyond the simple utilitarian level and emanates out of a real theology for the maintenance of female purity' (Boudhiba, 1982 pp. 49–50).

Today, millions of women in Saudi Arabia still wear the veil. Whenever they venture outside their homes, they are draped in the 'abaya' (a long black dress that covers the entire body), their heads are covered by a hijab, and their faces are concealed by a black cover or veil. Decent dress forms an important part of good manners for Muslims. Islam has fixed a minimum level of decency for dress, mainly at times of prayer and devotion, when a woman must cover all her body except for her face, hands and feet. Wearing a 'hijab' is required when appearing in society. The word 'hijab' comes from the verb 'hajaba', to conceal or render invisible by use of a shield. The hijab is meant to cover only the hair of a woman, not her face. The veil, or 'niquab' (mask) is a piece of black cloth worn over the face. It may conceal only the lower part of the face, leaving the eyes uncovered, or completely hide the face.

The dilemma of whether or not a woman should wear a veil is a critical subject in Saudi Arabia. For most women, veils have a moral, religious and cultural connotation. While some women argue that Islam is the reason for wearing a veil, others insist that it is more a question of values and traditions.

For one 34 year old uneducated woman, wearing a veil is just a result of growing up with it and getting used to it. As she expressed it: 'I don't just wear the veil ... I was born in it, and I grew up with it .... It is all a matter of customs and cultural traditions'. However, a 40 year old (elementary level) married woman with two children, said: 'I don't like it at all, and I wish the

47

custom could change'. Then she added: 'I think that the custom
was established here in Saudi Arabia during the Ottoman occupation ... I hope my daughter will not have to wear it, but society
still demands it'. A 32 year old woman with an MA in education
agreed: 'I do not think that it is necessary to wear the veil ...
Islam has never required us to cover our faces. It is not disgrace-
ful or dishonourable to show our faces ... The veil is all a matter
of practices and custom'.

For many Saudi women, religious connotations are associated
with a whole body of social and cultural traditions. The veil in
Saudi Arabia has become connected with a spiritual and religious meaning that symbolises the virtues of conduct. Most illiterate and uneducated women consider that not wearing a veil is
'haram' (taboo) and 'ayb' (shameful), as it may engender divine
retribution and social stigma among their filial group. Thus by
wearing a veil a woman expresses her deep attachment to religious norms, and her extreme reverence to the values and traditions of society. Religious doctrines and traditional norms have
become intrinsically united. As a 38 year old sociologist teaching
at the university explained: 'The veil is nothing more than an
inherited social custom, and it is not from Islam ... It is a combi-
nation of local traditions and an interpretation of religion ... It
has become something that is very difficult to dissociate from'.

Does Islam really require Muslim women to hide their faces
with a niqab or veil? According to the Qur'an, a female should
cover her body completely, leaving her face and hands uncovered:

> O Prophet! Tell
> Thy wives and daughters,
> And the believing women,
> That they should cast
> Their outer garments over
> Their persons (when outdoors)
> That is most convenient,
> That they should be known
> (As such) and not molested
> And God is oft-Forgiving,
> Most Merciful.
> (Al Ahzab, 33, verse 59)

This verse is directed at all Muslim women, not just those of the Prophet's household. It was a time of insecurity and women were asked to cover themselves with outer garments when walking outdoors. The Arabic word for an outer garment is 'Jilbab' which is a long gown that covers the whole body or a cloak that covers the neck and bosom. Wearing distinctive clothing that covered the body was considered a badge of honour and distinction as it protected women from harm and molestation arising from the social and moral decline that existed in Medina at the time (the Qur'an, Yusuf Ali translation, 1983, p. 1126). Other verses proclaim:

> Say to the believing men
> That they should cast down
> Their eyes and guard
> Their private parts; that is purer for them.
> And God is well acquainted with all that they do.
> (Al Nour, 24, verse 30)

> And say to the believing women
> That they cast down their eyes
> And guard their private parts
> And reveal not their adornment
> Except what (must ordinarily) appear
> Thereof; and let them cast
> Their veils over
> Their bosoms and not reveal
> Their adornment except
> To their husbands, their fathers
> Their husband's fathers, their sons,
> Their husband's sons,
> Their brothers or their brothers' sons
> Or their sisters' sons,
> Or their women, or the slaves
> Whom their right hands
> Possess, or male servants
> not having sexual desire,
> Or children who have not yet attained knowledge
> of women's private parts;
> Nor let them stamp their feet so that their hidden

Ornaments may be known
And turn all together to God in repentance
O you believers so that ye may be successful.
(Al Nour, 24, verse 31)

In these two verses the rule of modesty applies to men as well as
women. All believers were required not to stare at each other in
temptation, and to guard themselves against adultery. A greater
degree of concealment was required for women as during Al
Jahiliyya women dressed immodestly, with their necks and
chests uncovered.

There have been different interpretations of the words 'that
they should not display their adornment ['zeenah' in Arabic],
except what appear thereof'. According to Al Qurtubi, a thir-
teenth century Islamic scholar from Cordoba in Andalusia, the
Arabic word 'zeenah', which is employed in the verse, means
both natural beauty and artificial ornaments (in Al Qurtubi *Al
Ja'ameh li Ahkam Al Qur'an*, 1967)

Scholars and companions of the Prophet known as Al Sahaba
provided the following interpretations of 'what appear thereof'.
Ibn Massoud said that it meant the dress; Ibn Joubeir indicated that
it should include the face. Al Ouzaii' said that it meant the face,
the palms of the hands and the dress. Ibn Abbas, Quta'da and Ibn
Moukhrifa agreed that it referred also to the ornaments on the face,
such as the 'kohl' around the eyes, the bracelets and rings on the
hands, and henna (natural orange dye) up to the elbow.

According to Zamakhshary (twelfth century), in his commen-
tary of the Qur'an, *Al Kashaf,* the meaning of 'what appears
thereof' should include the face and the hands as they are essential for a woman's daily activities. A later scholar, Tantawi
Jawhari (died 1940), agreed that the face, hands, and feet should
not be covered, because that would constitute a problem for a
woman when engaging in business, seeking medical attention or
taking the 'Shahada' (religious oath) in front of a 'Quadi'
(judge).

In his book *Al mara'a fi al Qur'an* (n.d.), Abbas Mahmud Al
Akkad concluded that it is well understood from the several
interpretations of this verse that women should not cover their
faces. He added that the hijab did not prevent Muslim women

during early Islam from fighting with men, praying with them or conducting business activities with others (Al Akkad, n.d., p. 66).

It can therefore be understood that it is permissible for women to expose their faces and hands to people who are unrelated to them. Al Qurtubi added that although the custom was to keep the face and the hands uncovered, concealing the face was allowed among extremely beautiful women to prevent them from attracting too much attention and charming men. Thus a woman should cover her face only for fear of seduction and temptation. As a 36 year old woman with an MA in sociology put it: 'There are different interpretations regarding the veil. In Islam, some scholars have argued that one should cover the face .... Others reject that .... I think that it is all a question of how one interprets the verses in the Qur'an. Personally, I believe that cultural traditions are the main reason behind it'.

The veil was not imposed on the Muslim woman who fought in battles alongside the Prophet and nursed the wounded (Awn, 1983, p. 134). Muslim women never covered their faces in the presence of the Prophet, for example when they sat with him to discuss subjects relating to various matters in their lives.

Ahmad Al Fanjari (1986) argues that wearing the veil is 'abhorred in Islam'. He explains that:

1. If the veil had been approved of, then all women during the Prophet's time would have been veiled, which was not the case.
2. The Shari'a or Religious Law forbids women to wear a veil during the Hajj (pilgrimage), even though she is mixing with men, nor is she allowed to wear gloves to hide her hands.
3. The Shari'a orders all men wanting to get married to see the faces of their future brides.
4. A woman is not allowed to wear a veil in the presence of a 'quadi' (court judge) when taking the 'shahada' (religious oath).

As discussed earlier, historical data prove that Islam did not invent the veil. It existed long before and was known among the

Assyrians, the Arameans, the Persians, the Greeks, the Turkomans, the East Indians, the Jews, the early Christians and some Arab tribes. The reason behind veiling was social rather than religious and was associated only with the upper and more privileged classes.

The earliest example of veils being worn was by the Assyrians during the Babylonian period (around 1250 BC), when they were used to distinguish ladies and respectable women from harlots and slave girls. Lerner (1986) describes how veiling was established in Babylonia as an institution by the enactment of the Middle Assyrian Law, paragraph 40, which specifies that all daughters, wives or widows of a 'seignior' must veil themselves when they go out on the street. On the other hand prostitutes and slave girls were not allowed to veil themselves and were punished severely if caught wearing one.

In Persia, aristocratic and noble women started to wear the veil in public during the Hakamanesh dynasty, which ruled following unification of the various kingdoms in the Persian empire around 500 BC. 'These royal women were secluded from men and were carried in carriages, hidden from public view by a tent-like cover or a curtain' (Sherif, 1987, pp. 151–63).

In India, women wore veils when outside the confines of the 'zenana' (their private apartments). In ancient Greece, at Thebes, women wore a mask made out of a piece of cloth pierced with two holes. In Cyprus, statues of veiled women have been found dating back to the eleventh century BC. Jews were also veiled, specifically virgins and married women (matrons). The early Christians used a veil, and many of those joining convents were required to wear some form of veil (El-Khayat-Bennai, 1985, p. 25).

The veil was introduced into Arab society during the Abbassid period (eleventh century AD) in order to distinguish between free honourable women and slaves. Ali Mazahery (1951, p. 20) argues that 'the veil was adopted only by idle women, i.e. women of a wealthy milieu, and thus it did not indicate a religion, but a social class'. Hatem describes how during the Memluks, upper- and middle-class women were the only groups to be secluded and veiled. She adds that Ethiopian and Turko-Circassian slaves were also veiled as they were considered valuable property of men. She says that later on veiling was extended to free women 'for fear that their chastity would be endangered and with it the family honour. Virginity had not been particularly important in the decision to purchase or to marry a slave, but it was of central concern in marrying a free woman' (Hatem, 1986, p. 26).

Today in Saudi Arabia the veil plays a major role in relations between men and women in traditional society. For a woman, the veil functions as a protective shield from the eyes of males outside the circle of her kinsmen. A woman is not supposed to wear a veil in front of those who are closely related to her (brother, son, father, uncle, grandfather). However, she may cover her face in the presence of a first cousin (paternal or maternal) as the possibility of marriage exists. According to AlTorki, veiling becomes functional for 'the maintenance of patrilateral cousin marriage patterns' (AlTorki, 1986, p. 36).

Saudi women wear a veil when outside the home so as not to draw attention to themselves, thus preserving their anonymity. At the same time it protects them from the attention of the opposite sex. For one educated 26 year old, wearing a veil is synonymous with being a decent and respectable woman. As she put it: 'If I were to leave my pretty face uncovered it would be like asking a man to come and follow me .... That is why I wear a veil.' For this woman and others the veil is linked to elements of chastity, purity and decency. It acts as a safeguard, a means of security and a defence mechanism for the preservation of family honour. The veil has become a symbol of social distance and protection of Saudi women from unrelated men.

Chatty argues that women's dress in the Middle East plays a vital role in social control. She explains how women 'are regarded by their societies as major repositories of the honour of the family [and] they are regarded as something sacred to be protected from desecration ... a modesty code can be said to operate' (Chatty, 1980, p. 403). Dodd argues that the garment an Arab woman wears is associated with protection of the 'Ird' (honour and reputation of a woman). He defines the veil as 'a means of maintaining interpersonal distance essential to "Ird", under circumstances where a woman might be exposed to encounters with non-kin males' (1973, p. 49).

In Saudi Arabia the decision to wear a veil also depends on the head of the household, that is, the father or the husband. His feelings on the subject govern whether a woman feels obliged to wear a veil or is free to choose not to cover her face.

According to Murdock (1965, p. 273), 'Arab society enforces sexual rules by external precautionary safeguards such as avoidance rules'. The veil is therefore considered an external protective device in preserving premarital and marital chastity, a means of preventing 'fitnah' (from the verb 'fatana', meaning to seduce, to lead into temptation). Fitnah refers to the fascination and sexual attraction felt by a man at the sight of a pretty woman. He may become distracted or demented (maftoun) and may even lose his self-control. An illiterate 26 year old, married with five children, describes it this way: 'You know, a man may feel tempted when looking at a woman's face especially if she is very pretty ... That is why the face of a woman is in itself a fitnah, an element of seduction'.

Mernissi compares the classical Islamic concept of sex to the Freudian notion of 'libido', or of raw instinct as a source of energy. She argues that 'a woman is endowed with a fatal attraction which erodes the male's will to resist her and reduces him to a passive role' (Mernissi, 1975, p. 11). A woman is therefore 'fitnah' as she holds the power of female sexuality and is a dangerous distraction for men. Fitnah would thus lead to chaos provoked by sexual disorder.

According to Sherif, a woman's veil is necessary because it 'reduces sexual tension in public places, frees her from the competition of being sexually appealing, negates her image as a sex object and attenuates differences in wealth and/or physical attractiveness' (Sherif, 1987, p. 153). As an illiterate 38 year old married woman with five children put it: 'A woman is from head to toe an element of provocation for a man. She should always wear a long dress and keep her head and face covered with a veil'.

For another illiterate woman (26 years old, married with five children), fitnah starts with the lustful looks men direct at women. She explained: 'Everything is in the eyes ... It is all in the way a man looks at a woman. This look may be in itself alluring, and it would lead unquestionably to adultery'. Islam strongly recommends both men and women not to stare at a person in an immodest way but to cast down their eyes as the look in itself can be sexually alluring:

> Say to the believing men
> That they should cast down their eyes
> And guard their private parts;
> That is purer for them [...]
> (Al Nour, 24, verse 30)

> And say to the believing women.
> That they should cast down their eyes [...]
> (Al Nour, 24, verse 31)

This defines the Muslim concept of 'the illicit look' (*Al Nazar al mubah*) as opposed to the 'zina of the eye' (*zina al ayni*), as the eye itself may commit adultery by the look it gives to a person with sexual envy. In a Hadith, the Prophet said 'the zina of the eye is the look; the zina of the hand is the touch; the zina of the tongue is the word; the zina of the feet is to walk following our desires, and the zina of the mouth is the kiss' (Musnad Ahmad).

The Shari'a enforces the existing social regulations regarding fitnah for the protection of the family from zina and for the maintenance of its stability. Any approach or temptation to zina should therefore be completely avoided. Veiling is perceived as being functional for the community as it maintains social distance between men and women and works against the disintegration of the family.

Qassim Amin (1925), promoter of the Muslim feminist movement, encouraged women to discard the veil in Egypt and insisted on the religious hijab which keeps the face and the palms uncovered. According to him, women control their sexual impulses better than men do. Men are the weaker sex, and thus should veil themselves. Amin argues:

If what men fear is that women might succumb to their masculine attraction, why did not they institute veils for themselves? Did men think that their ability to fight temptation was weaker than women's? Are men considered less able than women

to control themselves and resist their sexual impulse? ...
Preventing women from showing themselves unveiled
expresses men's fear of losing control over their minds and
falling prey to 'fitnah' whenever they are confronted with a
non-veiled woman. The implications of such an institution
leads one to think that women are believed to be better
equipped in this respect than men ... (Amin, 1925, p. 65).

For other women in Saudi Arabia, wearing the veil is a symbol
of a nationalist trend, a coded message that reflects an ideological choice. As a form of protection rather than a sign of oppression, the veil is viewed by some as an element of Islamisation
that symbolises Muslim women as opposed to non-Muslim
women. It is also seen as a quest for a more meaningful Saudi
identity. Powell (1982, p. 145) argues that veils are used by
women as a form of identification that they are Muslims. Indeed,
the veil is functional in creating a bond between members of the
Islamic community, joining them into a cohesive unit.

A 35 year old teacher, married with two children and holding a
BA in education from the United States, said: 'Yes, I wear the
veil out of conviction'. 'On what do you base your conviction?' I
asked. 'I am attached to my traditions. Wearing a veil is part of
one's identity of being a Saudi woman. It is a definite proof of
one's identification with the norms and the values of the Saudi
culture ... and I will teach my daughter also to wear it'. A single
32 year old with a BA degree from Beirut confided: 'You know, I
grew up outside of Saudi Arabia, but once back, I felt that I had
to wear a veil ... it becomes part of your identity'. 'How do you
feel when you wear the veil?' I wanted to know. 'I feel more
secure and protected from community pressure and male harassment. In a way it gives you a feeling of control as you can see
everyone and no one can see you, so you keep men guessing.
And today, as you know, for a number of Saudi women wearing
the veil and the abaya' has become a fashionable trend. It is very
feminine so I wear it and I love it'.

Some women wear the veil as a sign of defiance showing their
disappointment in and rejection of Western values and the emancipation of the West. Although these particular women have been
educated abroad and have travelled extensively all over the

world, they still wear a veil and insist upon its use by future generations. In today's Saudi Arabia the veil has become a means of defending traditional, cultural and Islamic values, a cry for the restoration of an Islamic identity against the intrusion of the West. Juliette Minces agrees that in several areas the wearing of the veil is perceived as a means of defiance against Western values, including the impersonalisation of the West and the slackening of morals among Western women (Minces, 1980, p. 70).

For one 29 year old single woman who has spent most of her life in Europe, gaining an MA in social sciences in London, the veil is not a sign of oppression: 'I think that it is very wrong to believe that the veil for the woman of Saudi Arabia is a sign of oppression or retardation or subjugation as the West believes ... and it does not mean at all that we hold a secondary status as all the Westerners want to believe. These are all false assumptions built against us'. She added: 'I wear the veil, because for me it is a sign of personal and religious choice. It is because I lived in the West, and I saw all the corruption and immorality in their, as they call it "liberated society" of illicit sex and drug abuse, that now I am more convinced of our local traditions and I am more attached to them. I want to preserve my Arab–Islamic identity, and for me, this is a way to show it'.

5 Education

Education in Saudi Arabia is the area in which women have experienced the greatest progress. The widespread availability of female education that came with the oil boom of the early 1970s led to considerable development in the status of Saudi women both socially and intellectually. Education gave Saudi women knowledge, skills and a way of recognising – but not necessarily exercising – their own social and economic power in society. As a 36 year old single woman with an MA in sociology put it: 'Education opened my eyes, widened my horizons and made me feel that I am a real human being able to understand and communicate with others ... it also made me a better thinker, and a better person whom people respect.'

Women's education in Saudi Arabia is a recent phenomenon. Before the discovery of oil in the 1930s, illiteracy prevailed among the population of the Arabian peninsula. Tribal warfare was endemic throughout the country, which was isolated from exposure to the scientific and technological advances of the West. In fact, as Catherine Parsinnen explains, it was mainly

> due to geographic inaccessibility and its former relative lack of strategic importance, [that] Saudi Arabia was effectively quarantined from any interaction with the international community, and particularly with the Western world. Great Britain was disinterested in establishing any imperial presence in what is now Saudi Arabia, and essentially pursued a policy of benign neglect, so long as the tribes of Arabia did not jeopardise its vested interests in Iraq, Kuwait, Aden, Yemen and the Crucial coast Protectorates (Parsinnen, 1980, p. 155).

The Ottomans dominated the whole area, especially the province of Al Hijaz, which is home to the two holy mosques of Meccah and Medinah. In 1880, they established a system of state schools exclusively for boys at the elementary and intermediate levels. These schools were mainly designed to serve the children of Turkish soldiers and officials, and classes were given only in Turkish by Turkish teachers. In addition there were a few private schools sponsored by individual benefactors that were spreading Islamic and Arabic teachings. Public education for girls was non existent as females were kept at home under the authority of fathers or husbands. Girls' education was therefore restricted to the home, where an old sheikh would teach them how to read the Qur'an and the basics of writing.

The first Directorate of Education was formed in 1926 in order to supervise the private schools and to create a system of government-supported education for boys only. 'At that time, the whole country had only twelve regular schools, eight public and four private, mostly at the elementary level and all in the Western Province (Al Hijaz); The total enrolment was approximately 700 pupils' (Al Baadi, 1982, p. 63).

It was only after the establishment of a united kingdom by Abdel Aziz ben Saud in 1932 that serious attempts were made to institute public education. In fact, concern for education emerged only with the development of the economy as a result of the discovery of oil in 1935. The Ministry of Education was established in 1953, and the first public schools for boys were opened the same year.

Meanwhile, girls were still confined to their homes by the traditional norms of gender segregation, and they had very little exposure to the outside world. Because of their biological constitution and maternal function, girls were considered unsuited for any kind of formal education. Middle-class families were the first to enrol their daughters abroad in the boarding schools of Egypt and Lebanon. Soraya AlTorki (1977) describes how education and travel contributed to the first changes in the traditional role of women in Saudi society. She reports that:

> Men began to travel abroad en famille by the mid 1930's. At the same time they began to acquire houses or apartments in other Arab countries, especially in Egypt, which then enabled their families to live abroad for several months of the year. Such prolonged residence outside Saudi Arabia necessarily exposed the women to a style of life much unlike that to which they are accustomed at home ... Since Saudi Arabia did not establish the first public schools for girls before the early 1960s, families who ... wanted their daughters to be educated

had to send them abroad mainly to Egypt and Lebanon. The families' prolonged residence in these countries favored this trend and their decision to keep their daughters in boarding schools was a likely consequence, which, during the last two decades, enabled some girls to continue their education through college and even at universities (AlTorki, 1977, pp. 284, 285).

The 1950s brought an increase in popular demand for public education for girls in Saudi Arabia. A group of young, middle-class, educated Saudi men launched an appeal urging the government to establish schools for girls. They expressed their social dissatisfaction through newspapers articles and stated their need for educationally compatible wives. These young men, who had been educated abroad in higher institutions and whose number reached 600 in 1951 (higher education for men was not available in Saudi Arabia until 1957), complained about the ignorance of Saudi women, and their lack of modern education. They insisted that women's education was necessary to the family, the children and the marital harmony of the couple. Many of them could not find intellectually compatible Saudi women and preferred to marry educated women from other Arab countries (Egypt, Syria, Jordan, Palestine, Lebanon, Iraq). This led to the emergence of a serious social problem, with Saudi girls remaining single as the number of men marrying foreign women reached more than one hundred per annum.

It was only with the accession of Faisal ben Abdel Aziz (first as crown prince in 1953 and then as king in 1964), that considerable changes to the status of Saudi women were introduced. Faisal was exposed to the Western world from a very young age. When he was 13 (1919) his father, King Abdel Aziz, sent him as his representative to England after its victory in the First World War. At the age of 21 his father made him Viceroy of Hijaz. In 1930, he was appointed as foreign minister. He performed several diplomatic functions and visited the capitals of Western Europe, Poland, Russia, and Turkey in 1932. Faisal sought to introduce change into Arabia without abandoning the traditional heritage of the country. He insisted that all Saudis should be provided with educational opportunities within an Islamic frame-

work. In 1960, Faisal became the first to introduce public education for women. Prior to that (1956) his wife Iffat had founded
'Dar Al Hanan' (House of Affection) in Jeddah, the first private
school for girls in the kingdom.

Iffat, a distant cousin of Faisal, was brought up in a cosmopoli-
tan city, Istanbul, where she witnessed the gradual emancipation
of women. The veil was abandoned in 1923 and women worked
as teachers, lawyers and nurses. Upon her arrival in Riyadh in the
early 1930s, she began to respond to the needs of the people, and
shared with Faisal the aim that all young Saudi boys and girls
should go to school. When discussing the opening of 'Dar al
Hanan' Iffat said: 'My husband knew what I was doing, but I did
not embarrass him by asking his permission. I knew there would
be opposition. I decided to open the school for orphans, for no
one could object to this and people would feel it was justified if it
was for so charitable an object' (Waddy, 1980, p. 89).

At first the school took just 15 little girls, some of whom were
orphans and some children of servants of the royal household. A
new class was added each year, and in the second year, families
in Jeddah started to send their daughters to the school. 'The first
girl to graduate at the end of her secondary education went to
England to be trained as a doctor' (ibid., p. 190). Today, 'Dar Al
Hanan' is one of the most prestigious schools in Jeddah, with
1300 students, a new building, and a centre for adult vocational
training.

In 1960, four years after Iffat's pioneering venture in Jeddah,
the government opened the first official primary school for girls
in Riyadh. However, the introduction of public education for
women was accomplished amid great controversy and met with
resistance. The main opponents of girls' education were the
'Ulama', conservative religious elements who claimed that the
planned establishment of schools for girls would lead to the corruption of their morals and destroy the foundations of the family.
According to them, girls should be kept at home and protected,
and should not learn disruptive ideas at school.

Cases of patriarchal opposition to public education for girls
occurred mainly in Buraida, a very conservative centre in the
province of Najd, where a public demonstration erupted. The
schools were stoned and government troops were dispatched to

restore order. Faisal quoted the Qur'an to convince conservative elements that Islam imposed no barrier on the education of women, and that on the contrary, the Hadith espoused education regardless of sex: 'Seeking Education (Knowledge) is mandatory for every Muslim'. In another Hadith, it is declared that 'The rank of Education (Knowledge) is among the highest', and does not specify men only.

During the days of the Prophet, Women were taught Islamic religion and how to build a moral and dignified life for themselves, their children and society as a whole. The Prophet himself asked Al Shaffaa', an educated woman, to teach his wife Hafsah Bint Omar to read and write.

Addressing himself to the Ulama and the conservatives, Faisal said, 'We are all united in our loyalty to Islam. Now tell me what the Holy Qur'an says. Is there anything in it which forbids the education of women? ... If there is anything in the Holy Qur'an that prevents us from opening a school for girls?' They kept silent, and Faisal added: 'There is no cause for argument between us. As learning is incumbent on every Muslim, we shall open the school. Those parents who wish to send their daughters should not be prevented. Others can keep their girls at home. No one is going to force them' (Waddy, 1980, p. 190).

Faisal also convinced the male conservative element that education could help girls to learn the Qur'an, and thus become better Muslim mothers, able to teach their children in the future. At that time, the Ministry of Education was the only government agency to be responsible for educational institutions and it was only natural that it would be in charge of the supervision of girls' schools. However, some elements of the powerful Ulama, who were suspicious of the actions of the Ministry of Education, continued to resist the modern educational approach for girls. In order to obtain their goodwill, Faisal decided to work hand-in-hand with the Ulama within the traditional power structure. The roots of such alliances go back to the one that took place between Muhammad ben Abdel Wahab, the religious teacher, and the first Ibn Saud in the eighteenth century. Faisal thus appointed conservative religious leaders to head the education of girls. This later developed into the General Presidency of Girls' Education.

A royal decree was issued to confirm the compromise between the Ulama and the Ministry of Education. The decree stated:

Thanks be to Allah alone. We have decided to implement the desire of the Ulama of our great religion in the kingdom to open schools that teach girls religious subjects such as the Qur'an, monotheism, jurisdiction, and other sciences that are harmonious with our religious beliefs, such as home management, the upbringing of children, and others that are not feared to presently or at a later date introduce change in our beliefs. These schools are to be remote from any influences that might affect the youngsters' manners, healthy belief, or traditions. We have ordered the formation of a commission made up of the Chief Ulama, who are known for their protective vigilance of religion and their compassionate love for Muslim children, to organise these schools, establish their programme and supervise their good behaviour. The members of this Commission will be subordinate to ... His Religious Excellency the Grand Mufti Sheikh Muhammad Ibn Ibraheem Al Ash-Sheikh, who will select Saudi and non-Saudi female teachers whose true Islamic beliefs can be ascertained. To the new school will be added schools that have already been opened throughout the kingdom. They will all be subordinate in guidance and organisation to this commission under the supervision of His Religious Excellency. This formation, however, requires time to prepare the means necessary for the establishment [of the new schools], and we hope that this will be in the near future. Allah is the true Guide and there is no Power but from Him (Al Yamamah, no. 193, Year 7, p. 6, 4\23\1379 A.H., 1959).

From the beginning the education of women in Saudi Arabia had to be segregated and supported by the state. After affirmation by the Ulama that the education of girls was in accordance with the principles of Islam, conservative families started to send their daughters to school. Fifteen new schools were opened in 1961 throughout the kingdom, and by 1970 there were 55 (Kingdom of Saudi Arabia, Ministry of Education, 1974). In fact, 'in 1964–65, the number of girls enrolled at all levels was less than 50 thousand and almost 96 per cent of them were found in elementary schools, and about 4 per cent were attending intermediate and secondary schools. By 1974–75, the combined enrolment of girls at all levels grew to over 284 thousand which number was almost six times as large as that in 1964–65' (Gadi, 1979, p. 106). Also, during the 1982–93 academic year, out of the total enrolment of 1.78 million students, over 700,000 were female (Kingdom of Saudi Arabia, Ministry of, 1985).

Education is now available in every village, town and city, and over 800 communities have schools for girls. Recent statistics show that while in 1975 the total number of female students enrolled at primary level (6–11 year olds) in all schools of Saudi Arabia was 246,559 (male students numbered 431,244), it increased to 649,509 in 1986 (males: 810,774) (Unesco Statistics, (run date 11 April 1989).

In the 1988/9 academic year 75,852 female students graduated from elementary schools throughout the kingdom (compared with 96,297 males). It was estimated that the number of female students graduating in the year 1994/5 would reach 117,694 (compared with 151,217 males) (Kingdom of Saudi Arabia, Ministry of Planning, 1990–5, p. 334).

Other statistics reveal that while the total number of female students enrolled at the secondary level (12–17 year olds, including students at the intermediate level) in 1975 was 65,996 (males: 136,745), it increased to 185,902 in 1982 (males: 279,690) and 255,766 in 1986 (males: 398,436) (Unesco Statistics, run date 11 April 1989). During the 1988/9 academic year 69,054 female students graduated from secondary schools compared with 65,086 males. It was estimated that the number of female students graduating from secondary schools during 1994/5 would reach 111,402 compared with 113,544 males (Kingdom of Saudi Arabia Ministry of Planning, 1990–5). As these numbers show, it is only at secondary level that female students outnumber males.

In Saudi Arabia, the Shari'a, or religious ideology, is integrated in all education programmes. No fundamental changes regarding women can be introduced without the consultation of the religious leaders. The function of the education system in Saudi Arabia is to establish a religious, moral and traditional entity in the Saudi society.

The general policy of education in the kingdom is divided between two entities: the Ministry of Education and the General Presidency of Girls' Education. The Ministry of Education is responsible for all modern educational institutions in the country, including men's and women's universities. It supervises the education of boys (4–18 year olds) and attends to its responsibilities towards them. The General Presidency of Girls' Education, established during King Faisal's reign, is considered a ministry but is independent of the Ministry of Education. It is in charge of girls' education (4–18 year olds), and is still under the supervision and management of the male religious authorities, that is, the Ulama. It is headed by a sheikh with the same power, privileges and status as a minister.

The General Presidency of Girls' Education received US$1.7 billion in the 1983–84 budget, which accounted for over 21 per cent of the US$8 billion education budget (Kingdom of Saudi Arabia, Ministry of Education 1985). The schools and colleges of the General Presidency are spread throughout the kingdom (for example Meccah, Medinah, Jeddah, Abha, Bureida, Tabouk and Dammam). Statistics show that in Jeddah the number of elementary schools for girls directed by the General Presidency has reached 142 with 41,694 Saudi students. There are 53 intermediate schools with 13,484 Saudi students and 32 secondary schools with 9,352 students (General Presidency of Girls' Education, 1988/9).

The General Presidency controls all schools for girls in the kingdom, including all private schools, but not schools for foreign students, which are the responsibility of their diplomatic missions. Whereas state schools under the direction of the General Presidency are free, private schools charge a high tuition fee. The only difference between them is that private schools offer more extracurricular activities and include more teaching of foreign languages (English and French). In Jeddah the number of private schools has reached 53 elementary schools with 4649 Saudi students, 14 intermediate schools with 661 Saudi students and five secondary schools with 359 Saudi students (General Presidency of Girls' Education, 1988/9). Education policy, including the curricula for all elementary and secondary girls schools, the appointment of teachers and the provision of textbooks are all under the jurisdiction of the General Presidency. Its general objectives for education programmes are as follows:

(a) to give girls a clear understanding of their responsibilities towards their children, their own home, and society; (b) to satisfy the needs felt in Saudi Arabia for a body of women who would be capable of maintaining a balance between the changing patterns of today and the traditions of yesterday; (c) to ensure a flow of highly trained women for service in education and elsewhere; (d) to provide all girls with an avenue to higher education (Abdel Wassie, 1970, p. 36).

The education system treats males and females differently due to the gender-based expectations of society. In fact school systems in Saudi Arabia direct boys and girls into different courses by a differential tracking system whereby boys are taught to think about male activities and girls are encouraged to develop their future roles as mothers and housewives. The curricula in girls' schools stress courses that are suitable for the social and biological function of a woman in a traditional society. In addition to religious studies, Arabic and mathematics, classes concentrate on home management, childcare, sewing and cooking. In the late 1950s an article published in a local newspaper stated:

We want the state to establish schools that would teach our other half [women] the matters of their religion and life, and provide them with a female kind of education because we want to prepare them for the homes not for work. We want them instructed on how to manage their houses properly, on how to nurture their sons, and provide our coming generation with good manners and pride, on how to be the mothers of the future which we so optimistically look forward to (Al Baadi, 1982, p. 93).

In Saudi Arabia's gender-based system, family organisation represents the core of society. Girls are socialised from their early years to acquire a domestic role that fits their expected gender roles. For a Saudi girl, becoming a mother is the norm, the ultimate aim of her life. She is brought up to believe that she should strive to be a 'good mother', and that it is her natural duty to devote her time to her husband and children. Girls' schools institutionalise this mother role.

Places for Saudi women in universities are fixed for them. However, the fact that university places exist at all is a major achievement. Twenty years ago, when the first generation of girls completed their secondary education, a problem arose when some wanted to enter higher education. At first, there was general resistance from conservative elements who feared that if 'women [were] educated beyond the elementary level, [they] might have access to men's professions or become associated with them' (Al Manaa, 1981, p. 93). Pressure was brought to bear by middle-class families who were already sending their daughters to colleges and universities in Lebanon, Egypt or the United States. They insisted that the government should allow all girls to continue their education in their own country and that the government should not stand against their educational ambitions. The University of Riyadh, founded in 1957, was the first university to enrol young women as external students in the fields of arts and commerce. However these students faced difficulties as they had to come especially to Riyadh, stay with relatives, take lecture notes from male students and study on their own for exams.

In Jeddah, the University of King Abdel Aziz was founded in 1967 as a private university by a number of Saudi businessmen who believed that the area was in need of a higher education institution. It started with business administration and economics faculties. In the beginning the university recruited mainly men and only a small number of women. 'The first 68 male students were admitted Oct. 7, 1967, and in 1968, 125 students were admitted to the intermediate year (80 men and 45 women). There were ten female teachers responsible for the evening classes for women' (Halawani, 1982).

Only in 1971 did the King Abdel Aziz University became a public university under the Ministry of Education. A separate campus was set up for women. As education is segregated, the university adopted the use of a closed-circuit TV system so that women might watch some of the male teachers' lectures. Women students are allowed to specialise in medicine, natural sciences, mathematics, physics, chemistry, liberal arts (sociology, history,

English literature, geography, Islamic studies, Arabic literature), library sciences, business/economics, and home economics (nutrition, family and child education, housekeeping). Architecture, engineering and pharmacy, remain exclusively male subjects.

There are seven major universities in the kingdom, in separate locations, four of which women can join. These are the University of King Abdel Aziz in Jeddah, with its division in Meccah, Umm al Qura, the University of King Saud and the University of Imam Muhammad ben Saud, both in Riyadh, and the University of King Faisal in Dammam (the eastern province).

Statistics show that the total number of female students in higher education is continuously increasing. In 1975, of the 26,437 students enrolled in universities just 5,310 were female. In 1986, the number of female students increased to 50,434 out of a total of 130,924 (Unesco Statistics; run date 11 April 1989). In 1988/9 there were 12,819 BA graduates of whom 6,581 were female. Women represented:

- 63.7 per cent of graduates in literature and the Arabic language.
- 66.15 per cent of graduates in education and economics.
- 69.73 per cent of graduates in paramedical studies.
- 46.9 per cent of graduates in medicine.
- 16.03 per cent of graduates in Islamic studies.
- 28.57 per cent of graduates in agriculture (Kingdom of Saudi Arabia, Ministry of Planning, 1990–5, p. 336).

The prevalence of sex-differentiated education specialisation, is reflected in differences between the curricula in men's universities and women's universities, and in the availability of courses (as already mentioned, architecture, engineering and pharmacy are not open to women).

Eighty per cent of all the women interviewed, both educated and non-educated, insisted that women should be allowed to enter all fields of education in order to prove their intellectual capabilities in the way that men can. A 45 year old woman, single with a BA in economics, added: 'Why not? Women are not less intelligent than men. ... They can even be better students than men. ... They should be able to choose any subject they like.'.

Women's education is also in need of a general programme for vocational training. There are governmental vocational institutes, but only for girls training to become teachers or who want to learn to sew.

Centres for teacher training for women only, under the direction of the General Presidency, were opened in order to train a sufficient number of Saudis to replace the large number of expatriate teachers of different Arab nationalities. The first such centre, which trained teachers for the intermediate level, opened in Meccah during the 1960/1 academic year, and by 1969 there were 26 centres throughout the kingdom. Other centres to train teachers for the secondary level were then added. However both types of centres subsequently reduced their activities considerably and were gradually closed in several areas by the government, and a decision was taken in 1978 to replace them with six Colleges for Teachers' Preparation in different cities of the kingdom (in Jeddah there are still two centres, with 97 students in 1988/9).

The first college, the Kulliyat Mutawassitah lil Banat, opened in Jeddah in 1981/2 with four divisions of specialisation relating to Islamic studies; Arabic language and social studies; sciences and mathematics; and home economics and education. During 1988/9 the total number of students in the Jeddah college reached 536. Girls were each given a monthly allowance of between 850 and 1000 Saudi Riyals (US$227 & 267), depending on their field of specialisation. Training sessions are continuously given to all teachers in order to improve their teaching standards. As for other vocational centres, 19 sewing training centres have been opened by the General Presidency in Meccah, Medinah, Taef, Tabouk, Arar and Dammam. The first tailoring centre was opened in Riyadh in 1972/3, and the following academic year a centre was opened in Jeddah with 64 students.

Other opportunities for vocational training are limited because of the General Presidency's policy. When discussing this matter with both educated and non-educated women, all fully agreed that Saudi women were in great need of many kinds of vocational training. One of them explained: 'Not all women want to go to university ... they may want to work on their own for additional income, maybe to help the family ... but the problem is that our society does not yet look in a respectful way at menial jobs' (BA, 35 years old, married, four children).

Most women suggested that Saudi women are in great need of instruction in crafts, typing, knitting, hairdressing, small electrical jobs, computer work, photography and beauty work, and also that factories should be opened for women to work in. Private women's welfare societies in the major cities do provide a little vocational training. In Jeddah I visited two welfare associations centres where courses are held in typing, weaving, sewing, embroidery, languages and other manual work. In addition, lectures are offered on religious topics, nutrition and childcare. As these societies are private, the government contributes only partly to their budgets. Also in Jeddah, the Dar Al Hanan high school, which was the first school for girls to be established by Queen Iffat, is starting the first Saudi private vocational institute for girls. The programme, which is in coordination with the American University in Cairo, will offer subjects such as typing, English, English–Arabic translation, accounting and computer accounting.

The programme is designed for women with high school or college qualifications who want to improve their practical skills. Mrs Rouchdy, general director of Dar Al Hanan school, commented:

> There is a big need for the girls to study skills that the University is not offering ... A graduate of King Abdel Aziz University in Economics or Public Administration, for example, knows only the theories on the subject she has studied. She has no practical skills to work with, not even in a Bank. In a Bank, she should at least be able to operate a computer but this is not something she has learned at the University. This is the gap we are trying to fill ...

> Another thing we are lacking are skilled Saudi typists, secretaries, and even telephone operators. In all the schools and hospitals where women are employed, these jobs go to non-Saudis. If we say that we want to 'Saudize' jobs and minimize the number of imported employees, we have to train replacements correctly and properly. Where are we going to get replacements if we don't start training them from now? (*Arab News*, 16 February 1989, p. 9).

The government has been very active in promoting and building schools and universities and encouraging education for all. For example education is free in Saudi Arabia and all women university students receive a monthly allowance. The sum varies according to the field of specialisation: SAR 1000 (US$267) for those in medicine, sciences and accounting, and SAR 850 (US$227) for those in liberal arts.

Reforming the education system is now one of the major objectives of the government. Article 1/12 in the Fifth Year Development Plan for the years 1990–5 states that qualitative measures are to be taken by the government to improve the quality of education and increase the efficiency of students through revised administration and management (Kingdom of Saudi Arabia, Ministry of Planning, 1990–5, p. 320). Other measures will be taken to revise teaching methods and diversify education programmes.

One of the major recommendations made by officials to improve the higher education system is cooperation between all universities – at the moment each university functions independently from the others in both work and programmes.

The Fifth Year Development Plan also emphasises the need to establish a new, systematic, general plan for higher education that controls at the same time the quality of students entering the universities (ibid., p. 328).

In addition the government (under the direction of the General Presidency) has been concerned with literacy courses and adult education for women. It supports this type of education technically, financially and administratively. Classes usually take place in elementary schools during the afternoons and evenings. These schools enrol girls and women who are older than elementary school age, that is, from 10 years to 40 years and above. Statistics show that in 1982 the total percentage of illiterates in Saudi Arabia for the 15-plus age group was 48.9 per cent. Of those, 28.9 per cent were male and 69.2 per cent were female (UNESCO, 1988b). Today there are 1027 literacy schools for women in the kingdom with 62,114 students (*Oukaz*, 30 April 1990). Most adult education efforts have been oriented towards the cities. As more girls are illiterate than boys there has been a general demand for more literacy programmes for children, young people and women of all age groups, especially in small villages and Bedouin areas (Al Tamami, 1989, p. 7).

The first five literacy schools were opened in the 1972/3 academic year with 1400 students: two schools in Riyadh, one in Jeddah, one in Meccah and one in Dammam. The aim of literacy classes, as described in Article 181 of the General Policy of Education, is to teach students religious studies, reading and writing, and to provide them with a certain amount of moral education. The curriculum includes courses in the Arabic language, history, geography, mathematics, natural sciences and healthcare of mothers and babies. The adult education programme involves four years of study divided into two stages: a) two years devoted to literacy, at the end of which students are able to read, write and do calculations: b) two years of continuing education, after which students should be ready to take exams to join normal schools at the intermediate level. Those who graduate from this stage are each awarded SAR 500 (US$35) (Massirat Taa'lim Al Banaat, 1989, p. 357).

In Jeddah I visited a school for adults. There were 100 students whose ages ranged from 15 to 45. I attended a class session and sat at the back of the room, watching and listening to women in blue uniforms repeating parrot fashion the 22 year old teacher's lecture on the benefits of protein. According to her, that was the best way for them to memorise the given information. I did not stay until the end of the lecture as most of the students were very distracted by my presence and were not listening properly to what was to be repeated. The teacher had to keep shouting, 'Do not look towards the back'.

Later I had the opportunity to talk to a few of them about the reasons for their illiteracy. For one 23 year old married woman it was her father who had objected to her going to school. She explained: 'I was married at 17 to a man I had never seen before in my life, and then I became pregnant, and it was difficult to go to school with all the family responsibilities'. 'But why didn't you go to school earlier?' I asked. 'My father did not want me to', she said. 'He believes that education is only for boys, and that if a girl learns how to read and write she might start sending love letters to someone.' 'But didn't he object to you coming to school now?' I asked. 'No, because now I am married, and my husband, who is a university graduate, insists that I attend the literacy classes. I am very happy that at least I can now read the Qur'an.'

A 35 year old married woman with five children said that she had started to attend classes 10 years ago but could not finish due to heavy responsibilities at home. She gave voice to her feelings: 'You know, education is better than getting married ... once you are married, you have to care all day for the husband, the children then – about cooking, cleaning, washing and ironing. Believe me, marriage is a great ordeal and I will insist that my daughter gets at least a high school diploma before getting married.' 'Why didn't you go to school before you got married?' I asked. 'I wish'. She replied. 'But you know our tradition is to get married at a very young age, so my father married me to my cousin when I was 16. Before that, I stayed at home.'

A very bright girl of 16 told me that her father had at first refused to send her to school and wanted her to get married. As she put it: 'You know, the weakness of a girl lies in her ignorance, and her education is her only real strength. I told my father that I will not marry anyone as long as I don't know how to read and write, and honestly I do not really care about getting a husband because I want to study and then work, Inshallah'. 'And your father, was he convinced?' I asked, admiring her strong personality. 'Well', she replied, 'he finally agreed that I could come to this school, but we are still "negotiating" about whether or not I should continue my studies'.

Before leaving the school I spoke to the head director, who informed me that in addition to the actual curriculum, twice a year all students are given a lecture on general awareness, including personal hygiene, menstruation, sexual relations, and what is allowed and what is not allowed according to the Shari'a.

Education in Saudi Arabia has been a 'big leap forward' in broadening women's horizons. In fact, it has given intellectual satisfaction to the Saudi women who are beginning to wonder who they are, and what they want from life; it has also 'given them the tools to search inside themselves' (Blandford, 1976, p. 103).

Speaking about the kinds of objective education has helped them to fulfill, some of the educated women voiced the following thoughts:

Education has given me confidence in myself, in what I say and what I do ... It has also helped me to think, and I feel more independent (MA in public administration, 30 years old, single).

Education has opened my eyes to a lot of things ... You know, it gives you knowledge, self assurance, a certain sophistication, and a special way of dealing with others (BA in literature, 30 years old, divorced, one daughter, owns a clothing boutique).

Education has made me feel more responsible ... Getting an education, does not only mean going to school, it also means acquiring some culture by travelling and mixing with people in other countries (BA in political science, 40 years old, single).

While for some, education has given knowledge, confidence, self-assurance and culture, for others the impact of education has positively affected their personal and social attitudes towards their family. In fact a number of married women have found that education has changed their relationships with their husbands and children. Husbands are perceived more as companions and friends to communicate with, rather than just 'husbands'. Children are treated with more kindness and patience. As a few women described it:

A woman's relationship with her husband is very different when she is educated. A man shares with his wife the problems he has at work, for example, and she might even advise him about a lot of things .... But you know, we Arab women, we marry Arab men with all the complexes of thousands of years, we accept them and we try to live with them in a diplomatic way. ... But nowadays, once you are educated, and if you are not happy, you will not accept anymore, you just leave (BA, teacher, 48 years old, two children).

I try not to put too much pressure on my children. ... I try to understand their capabilities, and the way they behave. ... As for my husband, I communicate with him as much as I can in a logical way, and I try to create a non-boring conversation. ... It is very important that he should be open-minded, and if he is not, well this is another problem (MA in education, 35 years old, married, one child).

I try to be moderate with my children, I don't slap them, I don't use bad words, I talk to them when things go wrong, well I try to use my own judgement (high school graduate, 26 years old, married, three children).

Today, the education of Saudi women has become a synonym for their first stage of development towards personal autonomy and liberation from ignorance. Speaking about the constructive results that education has brought to the kingdom and its impact on Saudi women, most of the women I interviewed established a comparison between their present day status and that of Saudi women 30 years ago:

> Education has changed our society ... In the past, all women were completely ignorant, you know like my mother, for example, she does not know how to dial a phone number ... but now everything is different, the Saudi woman has intellectual enlightenment, mental strength, and she has also the chance to get out of the house and get a job if she wants instead of cooking all the time (MA in education, 32 years old, married, one child).

> Education has given the Saudi woman more value. ... Before, she was like a piece of furniture, she would stay at home and she could not say a word. ... Today, it's different, every girl goes to school, reads the Qur'an and writes. ... Myself, I am taking literacy classes twice a week, and my daughters go to school. ... One of them is now 15, and she has been asked for marriage, but I insist that she should first finish her secondary education ... it is a must (illiterate, 40 years old, married, eight children).

> Now the Saudi woman is more conscious of her role as an educated woman who can teach her own children and raise new generations. All families are now very keen to send their daughters to school, and are very proud if one of them is a university graduate. ... Even men, they look differently at a woman if she is educated, they respect her more (BA in sociology, 27 years old, single).

> In the past, a woman used to accept silently her submissive status. ... She had to wait all day for her husband and was a machine for producing children. ... The final word always belonged to her father or husband or brother. ... Now, at least if she is educated she has more courage to defend herself and to face her family. ... Also, she can better understand her religion (BA in education, 35 years old, married, 2 children, teacher).

Education has also provided Saudi women with a path towards further development. However my question to the women was whether education by itself was enough for the continuous progress of the women in the kingdom. A definite 'No' came as the reply to my question from educated women. According to them, education may be a vital element in the development of Saudi women, but other factors remain influencing considerably their status. As a 27 year old single woman with a BA in social sciences explained:

> Education alone cannot improve our lives. ... If local customs and values are deeply engrained in the life of a person, then a long time is needed before the mentality changes and new things are accepted .... You know, we need more enlightening and awareness about what constitutes social traditions and what is part of Islam.

When discussing this matter with a pediatrician, a 35 year old woman who was married with three children, she explained:

> Here, we are dealing with a very touchy subject. ... Education alone is not enough. Our Arab men should become more tolerant and understanding towards accepting us, all educated women. Men still cannot tolerate the idea of a woman being more highly educated or superior to them intellectually. They are still attached to the traditional view that a woman should not receive too much education, but that on the contrary she should marry and stay at home. We are not given the opportunity even with our education to stand equal to a man, and we always have to follow.

Her words reminded me of one young woman I had interviewed, a 19 year old single woman who could not continue her education because her father did not want her to. She said: 'My father did not want me to continue my secondary education. ... He told me that it was better to get married and take it easy. ... I stayed for two months crying at home asking him to let me go to school but he constantly refused, and I never finished'.

A woman doctor specialising in internal medicine put it: 'We all get an education, and then what? If men are not convinced of our education, I wonder why they send us to school? We as women must be looked upon as human beings and we must be given the chance to prove ourselves'.

In Saudi Arabia the family is still the fundamental unit of social organisation. Barakat describes the family as 'the dominant social institution through which persons and groups inherit their religious, social, class and cultural identities [and in which] every member is held responsible for the acts of every other member' (Barakat, 1985, p. 28). Thus interdependency, common sentiments and mutual obligations, are crucial elements for the maintenance of cohesion and solidarity between members of the family. Children in Saudi Arabia are socialised into family dependency and obedience to the parents, especially to the father who holds authority over all members of the group.

In a segregated society such as Saudi Arabia it is usually the mother or the sister who chooses the wife. In fact women hold power and exercise considerable authority in arranging marriages from within their own secluded world. A mother first selects a possible bride and then recommends her to her son, who has not yet seen her, by providing valuable information about her family, character and physical appearance. Mothers exert a strong influence over their male and female children even when they have reached adulthood. She is given high status and respect, not only because Islam has commanded that, but also because she has attained the most valued position – wife and mother.

There is a correlation between the mother's education and the child's personality. Al Qazzaz explains how the education of women is essential to the building of a new society, and how 'without emancipating women from the bondage of illiteracy no real political, social or economic development can take place'. He adds that several studies in the Arab world show that 'men whose mothers had no formal education are inclined to oppose the notion of granting women equal ... rights and equal employment opportunities' and that 'quite the opposite is true of men whose mothers attended a university' (Al Qazzaz 1980, pp. 7, 10–11).

For the educated woman, getting married has become a serious problem. Marriages are arranged, and the opportunity to meet eligible young men is difficult in a segregated society. According to the Fifth Year Development Plan, the number of women students graduating from universities is lower than those graduating from secondary school (Kingdom of Saudi Arabia, Ministry of Planning 1990–95, p. 326). In fact, at the first opportunity to get married many women university students prefer to drop their studies rather than lose out on a husband.

It is clear that young Saudi girls are subject to an early socialisation that increases their desire for marriage and motherhood, which brings with it the respect of their kin groups. Marriage for a girl is therefore seen as an affirmation of her maturity and adulthood.

Marriage in Saudi Arabia is a social rather than an individual proposition. It is a communal affair, an alliance between families, a consolidation of family ties. Feelings of love are expected to develop after marriage, not before. AlTorki (1986), describing marriages in Jeddah society, explains how for some groups the joining of families through marriage is used as a way of increasing their symbolic and material capital. She adds that marriages also permit members of the community to establish and expand commercial ventures. Marital alignments also can have political consequences as those who are politically influential have the option of extending jobs and access to relatives by marriage (AlTorki, 1986, p. 145). Thus marriages are parentally controlled and family solidarity is strengthened by preferred intra-family marriages (to the first cousin, *ibn el amm*), as well as being a religious and social event.

My next question was 'Do you consider that marriage is an obstacle for further education?' Eighty per cent of both educated and non-educated women expressed their view that marriage should not be seen as an obstacle for further education. As a 40 year old single woman with a BA in social studies explained: 'It is all a question of willpower. ... When there is a will, there is a way, no matter what difficulties there are. Marriage should not be seen as a problem. ... If a person wants to study, she can make it even if she has children and a husband. ... You know, there are no limits to ambition'.

One 36 year old high-school graduate (married with two boys) thought that education is not an obstacle as long as the husband approves: 'I don't think that it is a big problem. ... It all depends on the husband, and he could be supportive if he wants. ... I was married at 14 when I was in elementary school, and I had two children so I could not continue. ... But then at 28 I went back to school with the approval of my husband, who is encouraging me all the time. I have been studying for six years, and next year I will graduate from the secondary level. ... I am very happy about it'. 'Is your husband highly educated?' I asked. 'Not at all' she answered. 'But you know he travels a lot for business to Europe, and he believes that women should be educated and should travel like a man, so he takes me with him every time he goes.' 'But what if the girl wants to continue her education and the husband refuses?' I asked. 'If she is already married, then she can't do anything, but if not she can put it as a condition in the marriage contract.'

In fact, an increasing number of girls are continuing their secondary education after marriage. Although parents are still marrying off their daughters at a young age, a number of them are now insisting on including a special clause in the marriage contract that allows the girl to continue at school after marriage. If the husband violates the agreement, the girl has the right to divorce.

It seems evident that the mixture of norms, beliefs and principles emanating from the patriarchal system are still exerting a considerable influence on people's lives. Education cannot in such a short time erode completely what has always existed. Local traditions and customs that constitute the cultural heritage of the country are cherished as precious and become a part of one's person.

Another factor that has influenced the education of Saudi women is the influx of money into the country. Oil boom revenue in the early 1970s allowed the large-scale development of the education system for both boys and girls. One of the largest education infrastructures in the Arab world was built, and the hiring of teachers from different Arab countries made education possible for Saudi women in a short period of time.

I noticed during the interviews that the motivation to obtain education was strong among illiterates, and especially among those with low incomes. Several women expressed to me their eagerness to attend literacy classes and to let their daughters pursue their education. As one of them said: 'I don't know how to read or write, but I want my daughters to go to school and to college, and then to become teachers, and let the man wait'.

6 Work

The participation of women in the labour market marks a major change in the traditional role of women in Saudi Arabia. The need for self-recognition and a desire for personal and financial independence has arisen among educated Saudi women and paved the way for their participation in the labour force. The evolution of the economic situation, including the continuous process of urbanisation, industrialisation and modernisation in the country, has also introduced new employment opportunities for Saudi women.

In Saudi Arabia the relationship between economic growth and employment has been a strong and direct one. Over the past twenty years the growth in employment opportunities has surpassed the number of Saudi entrants into the labour market, thus causing a substantial increase in foreign labour. In fact Saudi Arabia's population and the size of its national workforce has been insufficient to meet the total manpower requirements of the Saudi economy. The government therefore opted to import foreign labour to fill the vacant positions. Efforts were made to increase the number of qualified Saudi nationals through expanding the education system but the foreign workforce continued to increase at a high rate and the government eventually called for a reduction of 600 000 in the size of the foreign workforce, which stood at 3.56 million in 1989 (Kingdom of Saudi Arabia, Ministry of Planning, 1990–5).

The policy of the government is to develop a Saudi workforce by encouraging the participation of Saudi nationals in all sectors of the economy. The 'Saudisation' (that is, Saudi nationals replacing foreign workers) of the public and private sectors involves a higher level of participation by female as well as male Saudis. The Fifth Year Development Plan states that 'To achieve sustained economic growth and a significant reduction in the size of the foreign work force ... there is a need to ... increase the pool of economically active Saudi nationals by opening the doors to a larger participation of Saudi women in the labour force' (Kingdom of Saudi Arabia, Ministry of Planning, 1990–5, Article 6.2.5. English copy,

p. 23). Previously the Fourth Year Development Plan had stated that 50,000 educated women were expected to join the labour market between 1985 and 1990. (Kingdom of Saudi Arabia, Ministry of Planning, 1985–90, p. 83).

According to the Fifth Year Development Plan, from 1989–90 the Saudi female participation rate in the civilian economic sectors reached 5.3 per cent, compared with 54.4 per cent for males. It was estimated that by the end of 1994–5, the female participation rate would gradually increase to 6.0 per cent compared with 55.0 per cent for males (Kingdom of Saudi Arabia, Ministry of Planning, 1990–5, p. 29). In other words, the total Saudi national labour force was projected to increase by 478,800 or an average annual rate of 4.5 per cent, during the Fourth Plan.

The Saudi female labour force is expected to increase at a significantly higher average annual rate – 6.9 per cent – than the Saudi male labour force, which is expected to increase at an average annual rate of 4.3 per cent (ibid., p. 30). The number of Saudi females entering the labour market during the Fifth Plan years (1990–95) is estimated at 60,200 or 10.5 per cent of the total Saudi labour supply. Just over half of these women will be university graduates. In some fields of study, such as natural and social sciences, the number of female university graduates exceeds the number of male graduates. In these areas women now represent a major and underutilised human resource (ibid., chapter 7).

The question has been constantly raised about the participation of Saudi women in national development and the issue has aroused great controversy. The attitude of Saudi males ranges from extreme conservatism to those who favour the gradual emancipation of women into the world of work. The debate on the legitimacy and definition of women's employment has become intense over whether women should or should not become active members of society. According to Islam a woman has the right to work and to earn money, but only if this is not detrimental to herself, her husband or her children. All Muslim women have the right to hold government positions or to work in commerce, industry and agriculture. For example Khadija, the first wife of the Prophet, ran her own caravan business in Meccah in the seventh century.

In Saudi Arabia the conservative elements are the 'Ulama' or religious leaders. Although they were the first to appoint women as teachers upon formation of the General Presidency of Girls' Education, the Ulamas question other work outside the home. Their argument focuses on the reproductive capacity of women and on motherhood as a woman's major goal in life. They accept a sexual division of labour based on the biological differences between the sexes.

The traditional roles of Saudi women have been defined and developed by society. By virtue of their biological differences, men and women occupy different social roles with different areas of work. Whereas men are seen as the 'breadwinners' of the family, women are considered to be responsible for the home, assuming the domestic role of wife and mother. Conservative and traditionalist elements argue that Islamic laws, social norms and local traditions have praised and defined the natural role of women as mothers and housewives. The first responsibilities of a woman are therefore to stay at home to care for her husband and children. Their assertion that the Qur'an has established that men should be the breadwinners of their households is based on the following verse:

> Men are the protectors
> And maintainers of women,
> Because God has given
> The one more (strength)
> Than the other, and because
> They support them
> From their means [...]
> (Al Nisaa', 4, verse 34)

The conservatives' view is that if a woman is successful in her role as mother and housewife, then she has provided society with her best service. This traditionalist approach is represented by Saudi men and women writers who condemn the idea of women working outside the home. The Saudi physician and writer Muhammad Ali Al Bar refers extensively in his book *Amal Al Mara'a fi al Mizan* (1984) to the physiological differences between the male and the female that account for the particularity and superiority of the male. Al Bar considers that the practice of women working with men in paid employment in Europe and the United States has created social and psychological problems among women and led to corruption, sexual deviance, the spread of sexual diseases and a notable increase in divorce. Al Bar insists that the participation of Saudi women in the economic world will eventually destroy the entity of the family as they will have to be away from their husbands and children all day.

Souheila Zein Al Abedeen shares Al Bar's view about the participation of women in the labour market. She condemns totally the idea of Saudi women going to work, especially if it is in a mixed environment (Al Abedeen, 1984, p. 80). Likewise Ahmad Muhammad Jamal, a prominent Saudi scholar and writer, argues that women should stay at home and take care of their families. He condemns the idea of women participating in the labour market as it prevents them from taking care of their families (Jamal, 1981; p. 54) According to him, women should work only in the fields of teaching, nursing and medical care.

A more tolerant and liberal view, mostly voiced through Saudi newspapers and magazines, demands that the employment of women should be encouraged. Liberals insist that women have a vital role to play in the economy. They argue that the two sexes are complementary and that failure to employ women will paralyse the development of society. Fatima Mandili, a professor at the University of King Abdel Aziz in Jeddah, insists that work by women is a social necessity as long as it does not interfere with their duties at home. She argues that women constitute half of society, and it is very important that they should contribute to the development of the country by working. Mandili says that the role of the family is to help their daughters to seek jobs that could help to improve their financial status. However, she concludes that most Saudi families are not yet psychologically ready to accept the concept of a woman working outside the home (Mandili, 1982, Al Medinah Al Mounawwarah (no: 5477)).

The Saudi writer and publisher Muhammad Salahuddin thinks that women ought to be employed. In a newspaper interview he declared 'It's a shame to educate our women and not have them make use of their education and brains. You can't send them to graduate school for Master's degrees and PhDs and then leave them at home .... Work is an extension of education and you can't have half of your society idle. This is a problem that needs a solution' (Salahuddin, 1989, p. 7).

The issue of defining and designing an appropriate role for women in Saudi Arabia, and the type and amount of work women could do, has become the centre of attention among government officials. King Fahd ben Abdel Aziz proclaimed on various occasions that Saudi women should participate in the development of the country and that job opportunities should be found for them to work in different areas, as long as this does not interfere with the Islamic Sharia'a. He also discussed the possibility of providing small factories where women could work even while still at school or university (*Okaz*, 25 August 1987, p. 17).

Sheikh Abdel Aziz Muhammad Tuwaijiri, the second deputy of the National Guard, commented that 'There is nothing in Islam that forbids a woman from working; in fact, the contrary is true. To arbitrarily prevent a woman from working is against Islam' (Powell, 1982, p. 140). Likewise the deputy minister of planning, Faisal Al Basheer, is on record as saying 'I do not think that there are any laws in the country that forbid women to work .... The problem of women's employment stems from whether women could work in those fields that society considers inappropriate from a religious and social point of view .... It is necessary to take ... into account the fact [that] we cannot change the customs and local traditions of our society, although we are in need of labour manpower' (*Al Riyadh*, 1980, p. 6).

Ibraheem Al Iwaji, deputy minister of the interior, voiced the following view: 'I think that all Saudi authorities and citizens agree today that a woman should work. But the question is: where should a woman work? ... and what are the exact limits of her work without violating the existing norms and social traditions ... We must decide which specific fields a woman could join without any violations of morality' (1980). Sheikh Hisham Nazer, the minister of planning, summed up the controversy of working women as follows: 'It has been agreed that the issue of working women has significance. But there could be an unending discussion on whether a woman should or should not work. Yes, she must work but within the bounds of Islamic Faith' (Powell, 1982, p. 140).

Female employment in the modern sector is encouraged by the government, and the status of professional Saudi women has considerably improved in comparison with previous years, when women could not work at all. A 27 year old woman who holds a BA degree and is married with four children told me that 'the mentality is better than before, because 15 years ago it was a real disaster, as no one accepted women working outside the house'. 'What is the cause of this change?' I asked. 'The education of girls and the development of the economic situation have brought changes in the social structure as well as in the mentality of most families, who are now more ready to let their daughter take a job and earn money.'

Women in Saudi Arabia can work only within fields specified by the government. As a 28 year old woman with a BA in social work put it: 'Opportunities for women to work here are available within limited areas, such as teaching, nursing, or with welfare societies'. The restricting of women's work to areas is due to women not being able to enter employment sectors that presuppose contact with men. Women are concentrated in specific occupations such as teaching or banking, and the sexual division of Saudi women at work is reinforced by the social structure and the education system. According to Sokoloff, 'the notion of sex-roles implies a culturally prescribed set of sex-linked traits that differentiate men and women in both personality and behaviour' (Sokoloff, 1980, p. 15). She argues that the labour market is divided into two separate labour markets that hold distinct jobs for men and for women.

Saudi labour law does not prohibit women from working in public jobs as long as men and women do not work together under the same roof. Article 160 of the Labour and Workmen Law stipulates that 'Adolescents, juveniles and women may not be employed in hazardous operations or harmful industries .... In no case may men and women co-mingle in places of work or in accessory facilities or other appartenances thereto'.

A woman in Saudi Arabia is allowed to work only if three conditions are assured: (1) care of her husband and children comes first; (2) she works only within specific conditions that do not conflict with existing customs, for example she must not come into contact with strange men; and (3) she is restricted to work that suits her female nature, such as teaching, nursing and so on.

Today, most educated Saudi women wishing to join the professional labour market are finding employment in the following fields: the General Presidency for Girls' Education, universities, the women's division of the Ministry of Labour and Social Affairs, the Ministry of Health, the press and radio, banking and the private sector.

The field of education presents a large number of job opportunities for Saudi women. It is estimated that more than 62 per cent of working women in Saudi Arabia are in teaching. With the institution of the first schools in 1960, because of the segregation of the sexes it became necessary to have women to teach girl students. In the beginning women teachers were recruited from various Arab countries, mainly Egypt, Syria and Palestine. As the education system gradually became established and the number of girls' schools increased, the number of Saudi women employed by the government increased also.

The General Presidency for Girls' Education includes preschools, elementary and secondary schools, teacher training institutes and sewing institutes. The high administrative positions are held by male officials, but women do occupy other qualified administrative jobs within the schools. Sheikh Abdel Malik ben Duhaish, general director of the General Presidency, stated in 1990 that the number of teachers under the jurisdiction of the General Presidency had reached 80,000 Saudi teachers and 23,000 contract teachers (*Okaz*, 14 February 1990).

The General Presidency trains Saudi women as teachers and appoints them to positions at different school levels throughout the kingdom. Teaching is considered one of the most suitable and respectable professions, especially because it was the government that first established public education for girls. A major emphasis is therefore placed on the development of Saudi women teachers to replace foreigners and become responsible for the education of other Saudi women. An intensive programme has been set up by the General Presidency for the training of female teachers. Statistics reveal that in 1984–5 the number of women at teacher training institutes had reached 4,146 and a further 1,199 were attending tailoring institutes. In Jeddah the number of Saudi teachers at the sewing centres had reached 16 (General Presidency of Girls' Education, 1988–9).

In most elementary schools the percentage of Saudi teachers has reached 100 per cent, but only 84 per cent of teachers in village schools are Saudi. Although major efforts have been made to 'Saudise' all teaching positions, Saudi women are still reluctant to work outside the cities and far from their families. This is aggravated by the fact that rural areas lack public transport and adequate accommodation for teachers working away from home (*Okaz*, 14 February 1990). Nationwide, only 64 per cent of teachers in secondary schools are Saudi (ibid.) The percentage is low as too few Saudi teachers have specialised in biology, chemistry, physics, mathematics and the social sciences.

A 32 year old teacher with an MA in education from the USA and working as the head of a kindergarten in Jeddah said of her job: 'I have been in this school for the past six years and I find my work very interesting as I provide programmes for the children'. 'Did you work before?' I asked. 'Yes, just one year as a professor at the University, but I did not like it, so I took this job.' 'Are you well paid?' I asked. 'Well, thank God, my salary ranges between US$2000 and US$2500 per month, and you know we don't pay taxes here like in the United States.'

Women's universities in Saudi Arabia present another opportunity for educated women to be employed. They may be teachers, or may work in the administration. A 29 year old single woman with a MA degree who works as a teaching assistant at the University of Jeddah described her job: 'My field of specialisation is computer science, and I have been working at the university for one and a half years. I find my work very interesting and I like dealing with the other students, they are all like my sisters now.' 'How much is your salary?' I asked. 'Around SAR 6000 per month [1600 U.S Dollars (one US dollar = SAR 3.75)] and of course I have my own bank account.'

A 26 year old single woman with a BA in library science, who works as a librarian at the University of Abdel Aziz in Jeddah, said of her job: 'I have been working for four years in the library. I find it very interesting to deal with books, microfilms and students ...

and my monthly salary is good, it ranges from SAR 4000–5000. Every month I give SAR 1500 [US$400] to my mother, and I keep the rest to buy clothes for myself. My father also gives me money whenever I need it.'

The Ministry of Labour and Social Affairs is the largest employer of women in the country. In this sector, women hold middle administrative positions and run centres for handicapped children and vocational training, welfare societies and kindergartens.

A 28 year old with a BA in social work and employed as a social worker in one of the welfare societies in Jeddah, described her job schedule: 'I take care of poor women who come to this centre for nutritional aid. We provide them with milk, sugar, meat and vegetables twice a week during the morning. I also give them lectures on cleanliness'. 'Are you enjoying your work?' I asked. 'Very much. I have been working here for a whole year, and I like to meet other people. In fact I started as a teacher in one of the schools but I did not like it at all as it is very tiring to teach children.' 'How much is your salary?' I wanted to know. 'Around SAR 3500 per month [US$933]. I keep the money with me as I do not have a personal account in the bank. I buy whatever I need with it. As I am unmarried, I do not contribute to the household expenses, and my father also gives me money every month.'

The Ministry of Health is another sector that employs women. However the percentage of Saudi women entering the health professions is relatively low compared with other areas of the social services. Women work as doctors, nurses, midwives and administrators in the hospitals.

A 35 year old paediatrician at a hospital in Jeddah (married with four children) found the medical profession hard for a woman who has to take care of her husband and children. She complained: 'Regarding the house and the children, I always feel guilty as I cannot take care of my children. I don't advise any woman to become a doctor because men do not always want to help with the children'. She informed me that her monthly salary ranges between SAR 8000 and SAR 12,000. 'What do you do with it?' I asked? 'I share the financial responsibilities with my husband, so most of it goes on household expenses.'

I also talked to a 29 year old single woman with an MA in management organisation and working in a private hospital in Jeddah as a quality insurance director. Describing her job she said: 'My work deals mainly with the maintenance of the patients. I have been working in this job for the past five years, and I enjoy it as it is creative'. 'How much do you earn?' I asked. 'Between SAR 8000 and SAR 12,000.' 'Do you put it all in your account or do you give part of it to your parents?' 'It is all mine, as my parents do not need the money.'

There are four nursing schools in the kingdom where high school graduates are provided with practical nursing training (the first nursing school opened in Jeddah in 1964). The number of Saudi women graduating from these schools has been very limited due to the nature of the profession, which is considered undesirable. Nurses have to work in shifts at different hours of the day or night, and have to associate with unrelated men. Most families therefore still have a traditional opinion about nursing, and regard it as a servile occupation not suitable for a girl of good reputation. According to Alawi and Mujahid (1982) this attitude rests 'on the belief that nursing forces a girl to mix with men, to stay long hours away from home and to work night shifts: a job condition that is socially unacceptable and runs contrary to deep-rooted beliefs of what is permissible for a girl to do'. They add, 'what makes the problem worse is the high drop out rate after graduation ... after completing their course of study, many qualified Saudi female nurses prefer either to stay at home or take up an administrative job because it is comfortable, convenient and more rewarding'. Alawi and Mujahid conclude that in some cases the shift away from nursing is imposed by the husband who insists upon it as a condition for a stable marriage (Alawi and Mujahid, 1982, pp. 75–6). Therefore nurses are mostly recruited from the Philippines, Egypt and Ireland.

Saudi women also work in the media, organising radio programmes and writing articles for local Saudi newspapers on the subject of women. However, these women are not considered official employees.

Saudi women have also joined the field of banking. Since 1980 banks exclusively for women have opened in Riyadh, Jeddah and other major cities, employing more than 120 women graduates in economics, business and public administration (*Al Raida*, 1 August, 1982, vol. 5, no. 21, p. 7).

In Islam, women have the right to retain control over their own money, personal property and real estate. A number of Saudi women have substantial financial resources at their disposal and prefer to deal with it themselves. In fact more than 40 per cent of the country's private wealth is held by women (Bird, 1985, p. 37). The first bank for women was opened in Riyadh in January 1980 by the Al Rajhi Company for Currency, Exchange and Commerce. It offers limited banking services and all current and savings accounts are held by Saudi women. In March 1980 the Saudi–Cairo Bank inaugurated a new branch for women in Riyadh. Other branches opened soon after in Jeddah. In 1982 the number of women's branches throughout the kingdom reached approximately 13.

Women's banks offer similar banking services as men's banks. As a 28 year old single woman with a BA in business administration who has been working for four years in one of the women's banking branches in Jeddah explained: 'We deal only with women, and all the accounts are for women only. Women are allowed, if they want, to use the men's branches, but the ladies' branches do not cater to male clients'. 'But what if a man needs to obtain some kind of information?' I asked. 'Men are not allowed to come in to our bank, and if they need to know something they have to use the phone.'

Most Saudi women feel more comfortable dealing with other women and discussing their financial deals with trained women advisors. As a 27 year old BA in economics working in another women's branch put it: 'You see, women feel more at ease dealing with other women, and they can discuss all their financial deals with them'.

Women's banks also offer investment counselling and provide other related services that prepare women for a career in banking. The manager of the Saudi–Cairo Bank – ladies branches – in the western region (there are two branches in Jeddah) noted that there has been an increase in the number of Saudi women – whether working, divorced or widowed – who are handling their own finances without the help of a male partner. She added, 'Women's branches ... were created to help the female sector; to help them not only by giving them income, but to ... help them to invest their money wisely and make the best of their funds .... Now women are thinking about how best to invest their money, they are thinking about some form of income'.

Commenting on the new procedures that banks are adopting to advise their clients and train staff, she said: 'Women's banks need channelling and they need to train not only their staff, but their customers as well [because] the clients need to know what services to expect and ask for .... We are trying to establish a comprehensive training centre for both clients and staff [and] an information centre for women who are interested in knowing about finance, banking, economics, how to start up their own business, what they need to know in order to have a viable business and how successfully to ask for a loan' (*Arab News*, 11 February 1989).

In the private sector, Saudi women's employing opportunities are limited to either working in ARAMCO or managing their own businesses. ARAMCO, the Arab American Oil Company in the Eastern province, is the only company that employs women in general, and in particular Saudi women. It is the only sector in Saudi Arabia where women work in proximity with men, interact with them and drive their own cars within the compound. ARAMCO started to employ non-Saudi women during the late 1950s and early 1960s to teach at the ARAMCO schools or work in selected service and clerical jobs. In the late 1960s King Faisal issued permission for Saudi women to work there, but final approval was given only when parents gave their consent.

Today ARAMCO employs about 3000 women (1989 statistics) from different Arab and foreign countries (Philippines, India, Lebanon, Jordan, Egypt, America, Britain, Saudi Arabia). Of those, 2500 are single women. The women work in different professional areas, for example there are 1400 nurses, 600–800 of whom work in the medical field and allied medical services, 600 work in education and the remaining 200–400 hold jobs in the various clerical and administrative divisions. Out of the 3000 women only 300 are Saudis, half of whom are doctors or other medical professionals. Two hundred of the Saudi women are from the Eastern Province. Those who are married (100) live with their husbands; the rest are single and live with their parents, commuting every day. It is important to note that all unmarried Saudi women are employed only with their parents' consent. The majority of the Saudi women employees are college or high school graduates (mostly educated abroad); the rest are highly educated and work as doctors. Women who work in ARAMCO are paid the same as the men on the Saudi payroll, and receive the same benefits. In the past ten years segregation between men and women working in ARAMCO has increased considerably, for example women have their own office of work (personal interview with a director in ARAMCO, 2 February 1990).

Some women in Saudi Arabia own and manage their own businesses, for example small tailoring establishments, boutiques, hairdressing salons and private nursery schools. In 1989, 529 of Saudi women had acquired a permit to work in private business in Riyadh compared with 14,354 men (*Okaz*, 30 December 1989).

In Jeddah a 35 year old married woman with four children, who owns a beauty institute for women, described her experience: 'I opened my beauty institute two years ago. It has always been my dream to own a business. I travel to the States to get all the necessary equipment'. 'Do you earn well?' I asked. 'My monthly income ranges between SAR 8000 and SAR 12,000. Part of the money goes back into the shop and part towards household expenditure.

A 40 year old clothing boutique owner (elementary level, married with five children) reflected on her business: 'I have owned this shop for more than seven months, and I am very happy with it. I sell dresses for girls and women of all ages. I usually go to Europe to make the selection'. 'Is the business going well?' I asked. 'It depends on the month ... but in general my monthly income varies from SAR 4000 to SAR 8000 and I have my own account at the bank.' 'Is this your first business?' I asked. 'Oh no! Before opening this boutique I was working from my house, in different businesses. For example last year I was selling chocolates, and two years ago I was dealing with houserobes for women. But I decided this year that it was better to have my own shop ... You know, it is a way to impose your presence as a respected businesswoman in a male oriented society.'

Another woman (38 years old, elementary level, married with four children), who owns a tailoring establishment for women only said: 'I have been working in this business for five years. I first studied sewing and embroidery, and then I decided that I wanted to have my own business.' 'Has it been difficult for you to manage the whole thing?' I asked. 'Maybe in the beginning, but my husband encouraged me a lot. I have a maid at home from the Philippines to help me with the domestic work, and I have four women who work for me sewing dresses (two are from Thailand and two from the Philippines, and each earns about $ 200 a month plus food and lodging). But the most difficult thing is working with people, especially because most of my clients change their minds twice before finally agreeing on the style of the dress or the kind of embroidery to be put on it.' 'How much do they pay you?' I wanted to know. 'Well, for a simple dress, I charge between US$30 and US$100 depending on the style. Sometimes even more if it is a wedding dress.'

Sufficient financial resources are required for women's private businesses as well as a male family member (husband, father or brother) to act on their behalf when legal or business matters are required to be done with government departments. Other Saudi women working in this field participate indirectly in corporate partnerships, including business companies, construction, real estate, restaurants and investment firms. Women who work in the executive private sector are usually backed by influential male executives, for example a father, brother or husband, or indirectly by an influential person in the government.

Among these educated women I interviewed was a 35 year old married woman with three children and an MA in business, who was working as a senior manager in her father's company. When asked whether she was happy with the position she said: 'I have been working with my father for two years in his retail company. I enjoy it, although I sometimes argue with my brothers on some projects'. 'Are you treated like any other employee?' I asked. 'Yes and No. Yes in that I do earn an acceptable monthly salary (it ranges between SAR 4000 and SAR 8000), and I have to stick to my work schedule. However, as I am the only woman working in the company and at the same time the daughter of the boss, I am very respected, and I share an office with one of my brothers.'

Government efforts have been made to expand employment opportunities for Saudi women in both the public and the private ƽector. In the Fourth Year Development Plan suggestions were made by the government to establish new career opportunities for women in laboratories and in the computerisation of financial and official records.

The aim is to minimise the need for foreign labour and allow all sensitive information in government centres to be handled by Saudi women nationals (Kingdom of Saudi Arabia, Ministry of Planning, 1985–90, p. 83, Article 3/2/4). Small segregated divisions for women have been established in certain ministries, such as the Ministry of Planning, The Interior Department and the Department of Finance. The Civil Service Bureau is responsible for recruiting Saudi women for service in the major governmental institutions.

Statistics show that in 1989 the number of women working in different governmental institutions reached 75,000. Of those 35,000 were university graduates, 4000–5000 worked in the Health sector, 1000 in the Ministry of Higher Education, 350 in the Customs Authorities and 30 per cent worked for the General Presidency of Girls' Education (private interview with an officer of the Ministry of Planning, Riyadh, May 1990).

Of the 100 educated and non-educated women interviewed, 22 educated and nine uneducated were working in various areas of employment. One of my questions to them was: 'Why do you work?' For most of the educated women, working was a means of making use of their university degree. As a 25 year old woman with an MA degree and working in a business company put it: 'I want to use the knowledge gained through my education and feel that I did not waste all these years spent at the university'. Another said: 'The only way to complete my education is to work and see the result of my studies'.

For Saudi women, work is also an expression of self-recognition, self-achievement and self-esteem. As one of the women expressed it: 'I work for myself, for personal fulfillment, because it helps the formation of my personality, and I feel that I am achieving something'. Another added: 'I work because I feel

I will gain more experience of life and dealing with people ... it also gives you more confidence in yourself and self-discipline'.

Work also offers a certain degree of social status and prestige. As one of the women said: 'I work because I want to feel important in having a position and being able to help people ... you know, nowadays a woman is more respected when she works'. 'Why?' I asked. 'Because (a) she holds responsibility and (b) most men now prefer a woman to work because she earns money and she can help her husband economically' (24 years old, librarian, single).

For others, working is a means of obtaining security and personal and economic independence. As one woman said: 'Although my father gives me money, I like to feel that I am independent financially and that I can buy whatever I want without asking the permission of my parents'.

Some work because they want to help society and be productive in their role as women in the field of social work. According to one woman: 'I feel I want to present a service to my society and I want to help all those women who come to the association because they need a woman who can explain to them a lot of things they are ignorant about'.

Of the nine working women who were illiterate or had only an elementary education, three were working just to fill their time. These women came from wealthy families and did not need to work for money. However most of the others came from low-income groups (family income in the range of SAR1000–4000 per month) or – and worked mainly for economic reasons to help the family. Their work was restricted to simple menial labour, as janitors in schools or in welfare associations.

One of these women, a 19 year old divorcée (elementary level), described her job: 'I have been working as a janitor for the welfare association for four and a half months'. 'Do you like this work?' I asked. 'I am glad that I found this job, because I need to help my father, and as I am divorced I have to spend on my little daughter.' 'How much do they pay you?' I asked. 'SAR 850 a month [US$ 227]. I usually give all my salary to my father, and then he gives me according to how much I need.' 'You don't mind giving your money to your father?' I wanted to know. 'Of course not, he is my father. Before, he used to give me money and he brought me up ... Now it is my turn to repay him.'

A 34 year old married woman with five children from Rabegh, a small town north of Jeddah, discussed the reason why she worked: 'I work here as a janitor because I need money to raise my children ... You know, my husband is 63 years old. He used to work as a night guard in one of the buildings in the area ... But now he is sick at home and we need income for the children.' 'How much is your salary?' I asked. 'SAR 700 a month' 'Is it sufficient for you?' I asked 'No, but what can we do? This is our only source of income. However the government provides us with free medical care and free education.'

Most of the research findings regarding educated and uneducated working Saudi women show a positive relationship between education and work: the more educated a woman is, the higher the probability that she is either working or seeking paid employment. For example Saudi women who have a university degree are more likely to be employed outside the home, and they work more effectively than those who have only a secondary education or are uneducated. On the other hand, women with only a secondary education (high school) tend not to be employed outside the home and show no desire or incentive to work. Uneducated Saudi women do no work outside the home unless (a) they are extremely wealthy and can open their own businesses with the help of their families or husbands, or (b) they are in need of money and therefore have to work in menial jobs.

Although Saudi women show considerable enthusiasm for work, it is not their first priority. Women still prefer marriage as their first alternative, followed by the pursuit of education and finding a job, in that order. Another important reason for the lack of participation of women in the development of the country is that there is little economic incentive. As Saudi Arabia is now a wealthy country, thanks to the oil boom, most families are not in need of financial help. Similarly, as financial security is provided for Saudi women by their fathers or husbands, there is no need for them to work outside the home just for the sake of money (except for those who work as janitors and are in need of money).

While some Saudi husbands permit their wives to work outside the home, mainly to help out with domestic expenses, many still refuse to encourage their wives' professional advancement and exercise their authority to prevent them from working. A 50 year old illiterate woman who works as a janitor in one of the welfare associations described her work experience. 'I have been working as a janitor for more than 13 years. My husband is now 65 and he is sick and I have eight children who need financial help. In the beginning, he refused to let me work and to stay outside the home.' 'Why?' I asked. 'You see for us it is considered "ayb" [a shame] for a woman to work outside ... many men feel insulted if their wife works and earns money.' 'Does he accept it now?' I asked 'Myself, I do not think that there is anything wrong in working, and then when he saw that we needed the money he approved. Now with what I earn [between SAR 1000 and SAR 3000 a month it is a big relief for our expenses, and he does not say anything at all.'

A 25 year old woman (elementary level) complained to me that: 'I used to work as a security controller at King Abdel Aziz University here in Jeddah, and my salary was SAR 1600 a month. I was very happy, and my parents encouraged me, but when I got married my husband objected'. 'Why?' I asked. 'Well, he said that if a woman is married, and there is someone to spend on her, then it is better for her to sit at home and take care of the children.'

A third woman, a 29 year old teaching assistant at the university, explained: 'The work was my choice and I had to fight for it'. 'Why did you have to fight?' I asked. 'My father objected in the beginning, as he did not want me to work, so I took the application papers and I applied by myself without his knowledge, and when I was accepted I just told him about it and I took the job.' 'Why did he object in the first place?' I wanted to know. Smiling she answered: 'He said that I did not need the money, but maybe he was afraid that I would become too independent'. 'But were you not afraid of his anger?' I asked. 'Yes, but I was backed by my mother who gently convinced him that he should be happy that I am educated and that I have a job.'

For a 26 year old married social worker it was her husband who at first objected to her working. She said: 'My husband objected because he thought that my schedule was too long and he insists on seeing me at home when he comes back in the afternoon to rest. I tried to convince him that I was very happy with my job ... we still disagree.'

Other factors preventing Saudi women from participating actively in the labour market, are as follows. First, illiteracy is still very high among women in Saudi Arabia. Some uneducated women expressed an eagerness to work, but as one 35 year old said: 'I wish I could work outside the home ... A woman should be proud to have a job ... Unfortunately I cannot work, I am a complete illiterate'. An uneducated 27 year old, a widow with four children, said: 'I want to work but I don't even know how to write my name ... I think that every woman should have a job in hand, because she cannot guarantee the circumstances of life'.

Second, there is a lack of public transport for women. As women may not drive in Saudi Arabia, a male family member is constantly required to drive her to and from work unless she has her own driver. Certain companies provide their own transportation service for women employees, for example the Saudi–Cairo Bank.

Third, there are too few childcare centres where mothers can leave their children while at work. But even if there were enough, many husbands would still insist on their wives staying with their children.

Finally, there is a lack of systematic and organised training facilities. Women entering employment do so with no previous experience or training. As a 21 year old suggested: 'We need training centres we could join after the secondary level ... For example, a centre for public administration to prepare us for administration work in the government sector'.

In almost all areas of work the power lies in the hands of men, who do not delegate enough authority to female employees. For example the General Presidency of Girls' Education, the universities and the banks always have a man director over the higher committee of senior women that supervise the work of women employees. Also, men set the conditions and rules of work, and they understand neither the problems nor the needs of working women, especially those who have to combine their jobs with household responsibilities. Due to the system of segregation, any communication with the men in charge has to take place by telephone or in writing.

Although the government is encouraging Saudi women to participate in the labour force, women as an active force still lag behind in the development process. Furthermore, development programmes are more oriented towards the needs of men, who are considered the sole providers of financial security for the family. Therefore men are given more work opportunities than women. Complaints are voiced by women in newspapers and magazines about the need to make more job opportunities available to women. A high school graduate told one newspaper: 'If only those responsible knew how much we endure from the killing emptiness ... and the bad impact it has on us, they could save us from the suffering and the boredom ... If only they knew all that, they could take advantage of our education and labour in any field ... We hear a lot about job vacancies and the need to reduce the amount of foreign labour in order to give us more chances to join the labour market ... but every time we apply for a job it is a hopeless case' (*Oukaz*, 20 August 1988, p. 15).

Another woman (secondary level) added: 'The problem is that after completing high school, a girl cannot find a job .... She lives in an unending circle ... and the solution is to find jobs .... This is why it is necessary to provide training courses in teaching or the arts, or in languages, or in administration ... so that she could gain experience that would allow her to work' (ibid).

However efforts are now being made to promote the involvement of women in the labour market. In the Fifth Development Plan (1990–5) the government stated its intention to pursue labour market policies and measures aimed at enhancing the participation of women in the development of the kingdom. These measures are as follows:

1. To provide financial incentives to encourage women to start new businesses that are operated and managed by women.
2. To study the feasibility of opening a 'women's section' of the Chambers of Commerce, so as to enable women to keep abreast of new business opportunities.
3. To study the feasibility of establishing a venture capital company, operated and managed by women, through which women can channel their investment capital and obtain commercial loans.

4. To prepare annual 'Saudisation plans' for the gradual increase of Saudi women in public sector employment.
5. To review periodically the occupations in which the employment of women is deemed to be in accordance with the Shari'a in both the public and the private sector. This information will be dissiminated widely through the media.
6. To study the feasibility of allowing women to teach boys up to grade four at the elementary school level (Kingdom of Saudi Arabia, Ministry of Planning 1990–5, p. 37).

There has been some pressure to open factories for women and create new jobs in the ministries. The Saudi writer, Muhammad Salahuddin, commenting on this subject, explained: 'There are many uneducated women who are supporting their families and who are their only source of income; these women need jobs. We are talking about "Saudisation", this is part of it. They are thinking of employing women at the Ministry of Post, Telegraph and Telephone to sort letters. This is a good first step. We can find or create Islamic environments where women can work within the confines of Shari'a. The idea is to keep women productive and help them make use of their education' (*Arab News*, 4 March 1989, p. 7).

7 Conclusion

Throughout most of its modern history the Arabian peninsula has been shut off from the outside world. A central political power was absent, and the various tribes were in a constant state of warfare with each other. The Ottomans controlled only part of the peninsula – Meccah and Medinah – and it was only in 1932 that the entire peninsula came under the control of King Abdel Aziz ben Saud.

Some of the neighbouring Gulf states have always been populated by maritime trading communities continuously exposed to different cultural norms and patterns of social organisation. These communities accepted change more rapidly than the tribal nomads who lived in the Arabian peninsula. The port city of Jeddah, located on the Red Sea, was Arabia's major door to the outside world. The inhabitants of Al Hijaz are of mixed Muslim racial origin and have been more exposed to foreign cultural patterns than those living in other parts of the peninsula. Schools for women were opened in Kuwait and Bahrain before 1940, and the wearing of the veil was abandoned by the younger generation. While there are now many women's schools in Saudi Arabia the veil is still worn throughout the Kingdom.

In Saudi Arabia a direct relationship exists between Islamic thought and society. The social system is functionally related to various categories of religious and other thought, including religious ideology, tribal laws, local traditions and beliefs. Islam is the binding force of the collective conscience. It provides detailed prescriptions regarding the Islamic way of life, as well as setting out status, obligations and privileges of women. Moral and religious values are therefore the foundations of social order in Saudi Arabia.

Traditional authority is a characteristic of the social system. The legitimacy of this authority is believed in and justified by virtue of customs and rules. Traditional authority is vested in a power elite comprising religious and political leaders, that is, the members of the 'Ulama' from the Al El Sheikh family and the Al

Saud royal family. The function of the power elite in Saudi Arabia is to establish the general policy of the country.

The function of the education system is to establish a religious, moral and traditional entity in society. Schools are perceived as the major institutional means of socialisation to prepare young girls to assume their role as mothers and housewives. A major hypothesis of this study is that education has introduced fundamental qualitative changes to the traditional status of Saudi women. Major outcomes indicate that, to a certain extent, education has been a determining factor of social change for Saudi women. It has introduced qualitative changes to the personality of Saudi women, in the way they think and act, and has made possible the adaptation and harmonisation of the new with the old. It has provided them with knowledge, intellectual enlightment, mental strength, culture, confidence and self-assurance.

It has also brought about changes in the attitude of Saudi women to their families. Education has improved women's relationships with their husbands and children. Husbands are now perceived as companions and friends to communicate with rather than just husbands. Children are treated with more patience and kindness.

Education has given Saudi women access to outside employment in the modern sector. Data show a positive relationship between education and work, that is, the more educated a woman is, the more likely it is that she will seek paid employment. The concept of women working represents a qualitative change from traditional norms. Saudi women work to use the knowledge gained during their education; as an expression of self-recognition, self-achievement and self-esteem; in order to acquire a social status; to fill their time; and for economic betterment.

This change is however limited by obstacles pertaining to local traditions, norms, patriarchal values and social beliefs. Education may bring intellectual knowledge and mental gratification to Saudi women, but in the short term it may not change their defined way of life, their set of pre-conceived ideas or their beliefs. For example early marriage often prevents a girl from continuing her education. Marriage is greatly encouraged by the family, which is headed by the father or a brother who exert a strong influence on the female. Therefore marriage is not an individual but a social proposition for the sake of family interests.

Financial factors also play a role. The influx of money with the oil boom has made it until now, unnecessary for women to work in paid employment, especially as a workforce of more than four million has been imported from abroad to meet the needs of the economy. In addition, moral and religious obligations demand that women, whether married or not, are sustained financially by their fathers, brothers or husbands. For example, education is perceived by most of the educated women interviewed, as an element of refinement and prestige, an opportunity for enrichment of self rather than a preparation for work.

Islam in its purest form is not opposed to the emancipation of women in modern society. The Qur'an asserts basic equality between men and women by giving women equal (but not necessarily identical) rights to those of men, be they personal, civil, social or political, as well as in the pursuit of knowledge and work.

Religion and government are intertwined in Saudi Arabia. Sovereignty is based on an alliance between Wahabi religious men and members of the Al Saud family. Its roots go back to an alliance that took place in the eighteenth century between Muhammad ben Abdel Wahab, a religious teacher, and the first Ibn Saud (see Chapter 1). Today Wahabism is the official doctrine of the kingdom and is supported by the power of the state. Also, the Wahabi Ulama are incorporated into the administration of the state. Kuwait and Bahrain have adopted the Shafi'i, Hanafi and Shiite schools of interpretation, which are known for their liberalism. The rulers in Kuwait and Bahrain are tribal sheikhs – religious leaders are appointed by the government to particular positions, and have limited authority.

The wave of Islamic fundamentalism that has hit most of the Arab countries, especially after the establishment of the Islamic Republic in Iran in 1979, emerged in Saudi Arabia as a reinforcement of the Islamic identity. With the political turmoil in the Middle East and Arab disappointment with the West over the question of Palestine, young Arabs have turned towards the conservative teachings of Islam in an attempt, to find a solution to the social and political problems. In the process, the status of Arab women has suffered.

An ever newer national trend is growing in opposition to Western influence in Saudi Arabia as a response to conspicuous materialistic consumption and as a weapon to enforce the traditional way of life. Certain materialistic aspects of Western civilisation were easily and quickly adopted by Saudi men and women, and as a result stricter constraints have been put on Saudi women as a whole. In fact the reaction to the impact of Western civilisation on the social values of Saudi Arabia could be described as 'zealotism', that is, a state of mind and a pattern of behaviour that cling to the traditional way of life with great scrupulousness and rigidity in the face of the pressures of the Western challenge.

It seems evident that the status of women in Saudi Arabia has been directly or indirectly influenced by a number of several social and political factors. Today the coexistence of the traditional and the modern in different aspects of life presents a major challenge to Saudi women. The policies of modernisation in the kingdom, along with the rapid economic change, have greatly improved the status of women by providing education and job opportunities in the modern sectors.

The existence of women's groups, associations and economic networks is essential to the development of Saudi women's autonomy and to advancing their position in society. Public consciousness, in particular that of men, should be raised with regard to the importance and benefits of women's education. Women should be made more aware of just how important their education is when it comes to promoting knowledge among future generations. They should also be motivated to seek continuing education to help the development of their own personalities and their own intellectual and personal fulfillment. This could be done through the media and through lessons for both boys and girls in schools and universities.

Education should become compulsory for girls and literacy schools should spread out into rural areas where there is a heavy concentration of Bedouins. A programme for women teachers should be introduced to develop their skills and train them in modern education methods. Students should be encouraged to develop a new way of thinking based on critical analysis. At the same time, technical and vocational training should be introduced, especially for those girls who do not wish to continue their education after secondary level. Women should also be provided with training for office work and the chance to prove their ability in other major areas of work.

What is needed, then, is a restructuring of thought and analysis that accepts the fact that women are equal to men and provides the vital element for the development of today's society. It is essential to recognise the fact that Islamic values are not an impediment to the participation of women in the building of the country, and that cultural constraints placed on women should be gradually cleared away through education and public enlightment. Such reforms in mentality should start at home with the upbringing of the current generation of children, initiating them into the belief that any rigidity leads to intolerance, which is abhorred by the true spirit of Islam.

Bibliography

English and French Sources

Abdel Kader, Soha (1984) 'The Status of Research on Women in the Arab Region', in *Social Science Research on Women in the Arab World*, ed. Unesco (London: Dover).

Abdel Wassie, A. (1970) *Education in Saudi Arabia* (London: Macmillan).

Abu Nasr, Julinda (1985) *Women, Employment and Development in The Arab World* (Amsterdam: Mouton).

Alawi, Hussein and Ghazi Mujahid (1982) *Skilled Health Manpower Requirements For The Kingdom of Saudi Arabia: 1980–90* (Riyadh: King Saud University Press).

Al Azmeh, Aziz (1986) 'Wahabite Polity', in *Ian Richard Netton (ed.), Arabia and The Gulf: From Traditional Society to Modern States* (London and Sydney: Croom Helm).

Al Baadi, Hamad Muhammad (1982) 'Social Change and the Roles of Women in Saudi Arabia', PhD dissertation, Stanford University.

Al Hibri, Azizah (ed.) (1982) *Women and Islam* (New York: Pergamon Press).

Al Hibri, Azizah (1982) 'A Study of Islamic History', *Women's Studies International Forum*, vol. 5, no. 2.

AlManaa, Aisha (1981) 'Economic Development and its Impact on the Status of Women in Saudi Arabia', PhD dissertation, University of Colorado, Boulder.

AlManeah, Azeezah (1984) 'Historical and Contemporary Policies of Women's Education in Saudi Arabia', PhD dissertation, University of Michigan.

Al Naquib, Syed Mohammad (ed.) (1979) *Aims and Objectives of Islamic Education* (London: Hodder and Stoughton).

Al Qazzaz, Ayyad (1977) *Women in the Middle East and North Africa: An Annotated Bibliography* (Austin: University of Texas).

Al Qazzaz, A. (1980) 'The Education of Women in The Arab World', *Arab Perspectives*, vol. 17 (October), p. 7.

Al Saad, Nora (1982) 'The Role of Women in General Development in Saudi Arabia: 1975–80', Master's thesis, University of Minnesota.

AlTorki, Soraya (1977) 'Family Organization and Women's Power in Urban Saudi Arabian Society', *Journal of Anthropological Research*, vol. 33, no. 3, pp. 277–87.

AlTorki, Soraya (1986) *Women in Saudi Arabia: Ideology and Behavior among the Elite* (New York: Columbia University Press).

AlTorki, Soraya (1987) 'The Ideology and Praxis of Female Employment in Saudi Arabia', *Journal of South Asian and Middle East Studies*, vol. 10, no. 4, pp. 51–76.

Al Yassini, Ayman (1985) *Religion and State in the Kingdom of Saudi Arabia* (Boulder, Col.: Westview Press).

Al Zaid, A. M. (1982) *Education in Saudi Arabia*, 2nd edn (Jeddah: Tihama Publications).

Arberry, Arthur John (1969) *Religion in The Middle East: Three Religions in Concord and Conflict*, vol. 2 (London: Cambridge U.P).

Armstrong, Harold Courteney (1966) *Lords of Arabia* (Beirut: Khayats).

Ashley, Brian, Harry, Cohen, and Roy G. Slatter (eds), (1972) *An Introduction to the Sociology of Education* (London: Macmillan).

Assad, Soraya (1977) 'Role Demands of Professional Women in Jeddah, Saudi Arabia', Master's thesis, Portland State University.

Azzi, R. (1980) 'Saudi Arabia: The Kingdom and Its Power', *National Geographic Magazine*, vol. 158, no. 3 (September).

Babbie, Earl (1986) *The Practice of Social Research*, 4th edn (Belmont, Cal.: Wadsworth).

Badawi, Gamal (1971) 'Status of Women in Islam', *Al Ittihad*, vol. 8, no. 2 (September), pp. 7–15.

Bagader, Abubakr (1978) 'Literacy and Social Change: The Case of Saudi Arabia', PhD dissertation, University of Wisconsin, Madison.

Bahry, Louay (1982) 'The New Saudi Woman: Modernizing in an Islamic Framework', *The Middle East Journal*, vol. 36, no. 4, (Autumn), pp. 502–15.

Barakat, Halim (1985) 'The Arab Family and The Challenge of Social Transformation', in Elizabeth W. Fernea (ed.), *Women and The Family in The Middle East: New Voices of Change* (Austin: University of Texas Press).

Beck, Lois, and Nikki Keddie (eds) (1980) *Women in the Muslim World* (Cambridge: Harvard University Press).

Beling, Willard A. (1980) *King Faisal and the Modernization of Saudi Arabia* (Boulder, Col.: Westview Press).

Bennai-El Khayyat, Guita (1985) *Le Monde Arabe au Feminin* (Paris: L'Harmattan).

Benoist-Michin (1955) *Ibn Seoud ou La Naissance d'un Royaume* (Paris: Albin-Michel).

Bernard, Jessie (1982) *The Female World* (New York: The Free Press).

Bernard, Jessie (1987) *The Female World From a Global Perspective* (Indiana University Press).

Bird, J. B. (1985) 'Seeing Beyond the Veil', *Foreign Service Journal*, vol. 62, no. 1 (January), pp. 36–40.

Blachere, R. (1971) *Dans les pas de Mahomet* (Paris: Hachette).

Blandford, Linda (1976) *Oil Sheikhs* (London: Weidenfeld and Nicolson).

Blaxall, Martha and Barbara Reagan (eds) (1976) *Women and the Workplace: The Implications of Occupational Segregation* (Chicago: University of Chicago Press).

Bligh, Alexander (1984) *From Prince to King* (New York: New York University Press).

Boserup, Ester (1970) *La Femme Face au Developpement Economique* (Paris: Presses Universitaires de France).

Boudhiba, Abdel Wahab (1982) *La Sexualite En Islam*, 3rd edn (Paris: Quadrige, Presses Universitaires de France).

Boulding, Elise (1976) 'Familial Constraints on Women's Work Roles', in M. Blaxall and B. Reagan (eds), *Women and the Workplace* (Chicago: University of Chicago Press).

Bourguignon, Erica (ed.) (1980) *A World of Women: Anthropological Studies of Women in The Societies of The World* (New York: Praeger).

Bowles, G. and R. D. Klein (1983) *Theories of Women's Studies* (London, New York: Routledge and Kegan Paul).

Caesar, Terry (1984) 'Outside the Inside of Saudi Arabia', *The Yale Review*, vol. 73 (Spring), pp. 457–80.

Cave, W. M. and M. A. Chesler (eds) (1974) *Sociology of Education: An Anthology of Issues and Problems* (New York: Macmillan).

Chabaud, Jaqueline (1970) *The Education and Advancement of Women* (Paris: Unesco).

Chatty, Dawn (1980) 'Changing Sex Roles in Bedouin Society in Syria and Lebanon', in L. Beck and N. Keddie (eds), *Women in The Muslim World* (Cambridge, Mass.: Harvard University Press).

Chodorow, Nancy (1978) *The Reproduction of Mothering* (Berkeley, Cal.: University of California Press).

Churchill, C. W. (1967) 'The Arab World', in R. Petai (ed.), *Women in The Modern World* (New York: The Free Press).

Clements, Frank (1979) *Saudi Arabia: A Bibliography* (Oxford: Clio Press).

Cole, Donald (1985) 'Bedouin and Social Change in Saudi Arabia', in I. Saad Eddin and N. S. Hopkins (eds), *Arab Society: Social Science Perspectives* (Cairo: The American University Press).

Cole, William, and Roy Cox (1968) *Social Foundations of Education* (American Book Company).

Coward, Rosalind (1983) *Patriarchal Precedents: Sexuality and Social Relations* (London: Routledge and Kegan Paul).

Deaver, Sherri (1980) 'The Contemporary Saudi Woman', in E. Bourguignon (ed.), *A World of Women* (New York: Praeger).

De Gaury, Gerald (1967) *Faisal* (London: Arthur Barker).

Delcambre, Anne-Marie (1990) *L'Islam* (Paris: Editions La Decouverte).

Demourgues, Marie-Christine (1979) *Le Travail Humain* (Paris:Profil-Dossier, Hatier).

Djebar, Essia (1961) *Women of Islam* (London: Andre Deutch).

Dodd, Peter (1973) 'Family Honor and the Forces of Change in Arab Society', *The International Journal of Middle Eastern Studies*, vol. 4, pp. 40–54.

Doyle, James (1985) *Sex and Gender: The Human Experience* (Dubeque, Iowa: W.C. Brown).

Duley, Margot and Mary Edwards (eds) (1986) *The Cross-Cultural Study of Women: A Comprehensive Guide* (New York: The Feminist Press).

Durkheim, Emile (1985) *Education et Sociologie* (Paris: Quadrige: Presses Universitaires De France).

EIU 1993/94 (Economist Intelligence Unit Country Profile)

Fernea, Elizabeth W. (ed.) 1985) *Women and the Family in the Middle East* (Austin: University of Texas Press).

Fernea, Elizabeth W. and Basima Bezirgan (eds) (1977) *Middle Eastern Muslim Women Speak* (Austin: University of Texas Press).

Ferrandon, Marie-Christine and R. Jammes, (1978) *La Division Du Travail* (Paris: Profil Dossier, Hatier).

Gadi, Adnan (1979) 'Utilization of Human Resources: The Case of Women in Saudi Arabia', Master's thesis, California State University, Sacramento.

Gardet, L. (1970) *Islam, Religion et Communaute* (Edition Desclee De Brower, Collection Foi Vivante).

Ghiglione, R. and B. Matalon, (1978) *Les Enquetes Sociologiques: Theories et Pratique* (Paris: Armand Colin: Collection U).

Gibb, Hamilton Alexander R. (1947) *Modern Trends in Islam* (Chicago: University of Chicago Press).

Gorden, Raymond (1987) *Interviewing* (Chicago: Dorsey).

Grawitz, Madeleine (1981) *Methodes des Sciences Sociales*, 5th edn (Paris: Precis Dalloz).

Guillaume, Alfred (1987) *Islam* (London: Penguin).

Gulick, John and Margaret Gulick (1974) *An Annotated Bibliography of Sources Concerned with Women in The Middle East.*

Hadlad, William (1978) 'The Legal Provisions Governing The Status of Women in Some Arab Countries', *Population Bulletin of the United Nations Economic Commission for Western Asia*, vol. 14, (June), pp. 26–46.

Haddad, Yvonne Y. (1980) 'Traditional Affirmations Concerning the Role of Women as Found in Contemporary Arab Islamic Litterature', in J. Smith (ed.), *The Role and Status of Women in Contemporary Muslim Societies* (Lewisburg, Pa.: Bucknell University Press).

Haddad, Yvonne Y. (1984) 'Islam, Women and Revolution in Twentieth Century Arab Thought', *The Muslim World*, vols (3–4) (July–October), p. 137.

Halawani, Ebtessam (1982) 'Working Women in Saudi Arabia: Problems and Solutions', PhD dissertation, Claremont Graduate School.

Hamed, N. (1974) 'Muslim Women: Role and Responsibility', *Al Ittihad*, vol. 2 no. 3, (Spring), pp. 13–14.

Hammad, Mohammed (1973) 'The Educational System and Planning for Manpower Development in Saudi Arabia', PhD dissertation, Indiana University.

Harding, Sandra (ed.) (1987) *Feminism and Methodology* (Indiana: Indiana University Press and Open University Press).

Harding, Sandra (ed.) (1987) 'Is There a Feminist Method?' in S. Harding (ed.), *Feminism and Methodology* (Indiana University Press).

Hatem, Mervat (1985) 'Patriarchal Modernization in the Arabian Gulf' *Contemporary Marxism*, vol. 11 (Fall), pp. 96–107.

Hatem, Mervat (1986) 'The Politics of Sexuality and Gender in Segregated Patriarchal Systems: The Case of Eighteenth Century Egypt, *Feminist Studies*, vol. 12, no. 2 (Summer), pp. 251–73.

Helms, Christine Moss (1981) *The Cohesion of Saudi Arabia: Evolution of Political Identity*, (Baltimore: Johns Hopkins University Press).

Hobday, Peter (1978) *Saudi Arabia Today* (London: Macmillan).

Hussain, Freda (ed.) (1984) *Muslim Women* (London, Sydney: Croom-Helm).

Huyette, Summer Scott (1985) *Political Adaptation in Saudi Arabia*, (Boulder and London: Westview Press).

Iglitzin, Lynne and Ruth Ross (eds) (1976) *Women in the World: A Comparative Study* (Santa Barbara, Cal.: Clio Books).

Ingrams, Doreen (1971) 'The Position of Women in the Middle-Eastern Society', in M. Adam (ed.), *The Middle East: A Handbook* (New York: Praeger).

Jaggar, Alison and Paula Rothenberg (1984) *Feminist Frameworks*, 2nd edn (New York: Mc.Graw-Hill).

Javeau, Claude (1985) *L'Enquete Par Questionnaire*, 3rd edn (Paris: Editions de L'Universite de Bruxelles, Les Editions d'Organization).

Kandiyoti, Deniz (1988) 'Bargaining with Patriarchy', *Gender and Society*, vol. 2, no. 3 (September), pp. 274–87.

Kay, Shirley and Malin Basil (1979) *Saudi Arabia: Past and Present* (London: Namara).

Khadduri, Majid (1978) 'Marriage in Islamic Law: The Modernists Viewpoints', *The American Journal of Comparative Law*, vol. 26 (Spring).

Lemsine, Aisha (1983) *Ordalie des Voix: Les Femmes Arabes Parlent* (Editions Encre).

Lerner, Gerda (1986) *The Creation of Patriarchy* (Oxford: Oxford University Press).

Levy, Ruben (1965) 'The Status of Women In Islam', in R. Levy (ed.), *The Social Structure of Islam* (New York: Cambridge University Press).

Lipsky, George (1959) *Saudi Arabia* (New Haven: Hraf Press).

Lipshitz, S. (ed.) (1978) *Tearing The Veil* (London: Routledge and Kegan Paul).

Lorber, Judith (1985) *Women Physicians* (London: Tavistock).

Mackay, Sandra (1987) *The Saudis: Inside The Desert Kingdom* (Boston: Haughton Mifflin).

Mansfield, Peter (1981) *The New Arabians* (Chicago: J. G. Ferguson).

Massiolas, Byron and Samir Jarrar (1983) *Education In The Arab World* (New York: Praeger).

Mazahery, Ali (1951) *La Vie Quotidienne Des Musulmans Du Moyen Age:X—XIIIeme siecle* (Paris: Librairie Hachette).

McLachlan, Keith (1986) 'Saudi Arabia: Political and Social Evolution', in Ian Richard Netton (ed.), *Arabia and the Gulf: From Traditional to Modern States* (London and Sydney: Croom Helm).

McMaster, Brian (1980) *Living in Saudi Arabia* (Tokyo: Dai Nippon).

Meghdessian, Samira R. (1980) *The Status of the Arab Woman: A Select Bibliography* (Westport, Conn.: Greenwood Press).

Mercer, Blaine, and Edwin Carr (eds) (1957) *Education and the Social Order* (New York: Rinehart).

Mernissi, Fatima (1975) *Beyond the Veil: Male – Female Dynamics in A Modern Muslim Society* (New York: Schenkman).

Mernissi, Fatima (1980) 'Beyond the Veil', *Al Raida Magazine*, vol. 3, no. 12 (May).

Mernissi, Fatima (1982) 'Virginity and Patriarchy', *Women's Studies International Forum*, vol. 5, no. 2, pp. 183–91.

Mernissi, Fatima (1983) *Sexe, Ideologie, Islam* (Paris: Editions Tierce).

Michael, Mona (1979) *Images of Arab Women: Fact and Fiction* (Washington, DC: Three Continents Press).

Minai, Nayla (1981) *Women in Islam* (New York: Seaview Books).

Minces, Juliette (1980) *La Femme Dans le Monde Arabe* (Editions Mazarine).

Muchielli, Roger (1982) *Le Questionnaire dans L'Enquete Psycho-Sociale*, 6th edn (Les Editions ESF-Libraries Techniques).

Nabti, Farid (1980) 'Manpower, Education and Economic Development in the Kingdom of Saudi Arabia', PhD dissertation, Stanford University.

Nath, Kamla (1978) 'Education and Employment among Kuwaiti Women', in Lois Beck and Nikki Keddie (eds), in *Women in the Muslim World* (Cambridge, Mass.: Harvard University Press).

Nawal, Yasmina (1980) *Les Femmes dans L'Islam* (Editions La Breche).

Niblock, Tim (1982) *State, Society and Economy in Saudi Arabia* (New York: St. Martin Press).

Ochsenwald, William (1981) 'Saudi Arabia and the Islamic Revival', *International Journal of Middle Eastern Studies*, vol. 13, pp. 271–86.

Orenstein, Allan and W. R. F. Phillips (1978) *Understanding Social Research: An Introduction* (Boston and London: Allyn and Bacon).

Ortner, Sherry (1974) 'Is Female to Male as Nature is to Culture?', in M. Z. Rosaldo and L. Lamphere (eds), *Women, Culture and Society* (Stanford: Stanford University Press).

Ortner, Sherry and Harriet Whitehead (eds) (1981) *Sexual Meanings: The Cultural Construction of Gender and Sexuality* (Cambridge: Cambridge University Press).

Parsinnen, Catherine (1980) 'The Changing Role of Women' in W. A. Beling (ed.), *King Faisal and The Modernization of Saudi Arabia* (London: Croom-Helm).

Patai, Raphael (1967) *Women in the Modern World* (New York: The Free Press).

Patai, Raphael (1983) *The Arab Mind* (New York: Charles Scribner's Sons).

Patton, Michael Quinn (1980) *Qualitative Evaluation Methods* (Beverly Hills and London: Sage).

Pavalko, Ronald (ed.) (1976) *Sociology of Education: A Book of Readings*, 2nd edn (Itasca, Ill.: F. E. Peacock).

Peck, Malcolm (1981) 'Saudi Arabia: Islamic Traditionalism and Modernization', in P. Stoddard, D. Cuthell and M. Sullivan (eds), *Change and the Muslim World* (Syracuse, NY: Syracuse University Press).

Penrice, John (n.d.) *A Dictionary and Glossary of The Koran* (Beirut: Librairie du Liban).

Pietre, M. (1974) *La Condition Feminine à Travers les Ages* (Edition France-Empire, Collection Marabout Universite).

Pleck, Joseph (1985) *Working Wives, Working Husbands* (Beverly Hills: Sage).

Powell, W. (1982) *Saudi Arabia and Its Royal Family* (Secausus, NJ: Lyle Stuart).

Quandt, W. B. (1981) *Saudi Arabia in the 1980's* (Washington, DC: The Brooking Institution).

Qur'an The (1983) A. Yussuf Ali Translation (Beirut: Dar Al Qur'an Al Karim).

Raccagni, Michelle (1978) *the Modern Arab Woman: A Bibliography* (London: The Scarecrow Press).

Rauf, M. A. (1977) *The Islamic View of Women and The Family* (New York: Robert Speller and Sons).

Rehemi, Madani Faraj (1983) 'A Survey of the Attitudes of Saudi Men and Women Toward Saudi Female Participation in Saudi Arabian Development', PhD dissertation, University of Colorado, Boulder.

Reinharz, S. (1983) 'Experiential Analysis: A Contribution to Feminist Research', in G. Bowles and R. Klein (eds), *Theories of Women's Studies* (London and New York: Routledge and Kegan Paul).

Reitman, S. W. (1981) *Education, Society and Change* (Boston and London: Allyn and Bacon).

Rentz, George (1972) 'Wahhabism and Saudi Arabia', in Derek Hopwood (ed.), *The Arabian Peninsula: Society and Politics* (London: Allen and Unwin, Rowman and Littlefield).

Rich, Adrienne (1986) *Of Woman Born: Motherhood as Experience and Institution*, 10th edn (New York and London: W. W. Norton).

Richardson, John (ed.) (1986) *Handbook of Theory and Research for the Sociology of Education* (Westport, Conn.: Greenwood Press).

Roberts, Helen (ed.) (1981) *Doing Feminist Research* (London: Routledge and Kegan Paul).

Rodinson, Maxime (1961) *Mahomet* (Edition Le Seuil).

Rosaldo, Michelle Zimbalist (1974) 'Women, Culture and Society: A Theoretical Overview', in M. Z. Rosaldo and L. Lamphere (eds) *Woman, Culture and Society* (Stanford: Stanford University Press).

Ross, Patricia (1985) *Gender and Work* (New York: State University of New York Press).

Rugh, William (1973) 'Emergence of a New Middle-Class in Saudi Arabia', *The Middle East Journal*, vol. 27, pp. 7–20.

Salahuddin, Mohammed (1989) 'Saudi Women and Education', *Arab News*, March, p. 7.

Salameh, Ghassane (1980) 'Political Power and the Saudi State', *Merim Reports*, vol. 91 (October), pp. 5–15.

Saleh, Saniya (1972) 'Women in Islam: Their Status in Religious and Traditional Culture', *International Journal of the Sociology of the Family*, vol. 2, no. 1 (March), pp. 35–42.

Schatzman, L. and A. L. Strauss (1973) *Field Research* (Englewood Cliffs : Prentice-Hall).

Searight, Sarah (1985) 'Saudi Women: The Educational Revolution', *Middle East*, vol. 133 (November), pp. 37–8.

Shaker, Fatina (1972) 'Modernization of the Developing Nations: A Case of Saudi Arabia', PhD dissertation, Purdue University.

Sharpe, Sue (1984) *Double Identity: The Lives of Working Mothers* (New York: Penguin).

Shaughnessy, Thomas (1978) 'Growth in Educational Opportunity for Muslim Women', *Anthropos*, vol. 73, nos 5–6.

Shaw, John and David Long (1982) *Saudi Arabian Modernization: The Impact of Change on Stability* (New York: Praeger).

Shean, Vincent (1975) *Faisal: The King and His Kingdom* (UK: University Press of Arabia).

Sherif, Mostafa Hashem (1987) 'What is Hijab'? *Muslim World*, vol. 77, nos 3–4 (July–October), pp. 151–63.

Shope, Janet (1986) 'Separate and Unequal: Durkheim's Theory of Gender', a mimeo.

Sindi, A. M. and I. F. AlGhofaily (eds) (1982) *Summary of Saudi Arabian Third Five Year Development Plan: 1980–85*, 2nd edn (Jeddah: Tihama Publications).

Smith, Jane (ed) (1980) *The Role and Status of Women in Contemporary Muslim Societies* (Lewisburg, Pa.: Bucknell University Press).

Smith, Wilfred C. (1957) *Islam in Modern History* (Princeton, NJ Princeton University Press).

Sokoloff, Natalie (1980) *Between Money and Love* (New York: Praeger).

Stevens, John H. (1973) *A Bibliography of Saudi Arabia* (Durham: University of Durham).

Stowasser, Barbara (1984) 'The Status of Women in Early Islam', in Freda Hussain (ed.), *Muslim Women* (London: Croom Helm).

Tibawi, Abdul Latif (1972) *Islamic Education: Its Traditions and Modernization into the Arab National Systems* (London: Luzac).

Tomiche, Fernand J. (1979) *L'Arabie Seoudite*, 3rd edn (Presses Universitaires de France).

Twitchell, Karl Saben (1953) *Saudi Arabia*, 2nd edn (Princeton, NJ: Princeton University Press).

Van Dunsen, Roxann (1976–7) 'The Study of Women in the Middle East:, Some Thoughts', *Middle East Studies Association of North America Bulletin* vol. 10, no. 2, pp. 1–19.

Vattier, Guy (1976) *Les Taches Actuelles De L'Educateur Specialise* (Paris: Editeur E. Privat).

Viola, Joy W. (1986) *Human Resources Development in Saudi Arabia* (Boston: International Human Resources Development Corporation).

Waddy, Charis (1980) *Women in The Muslim History* (London: The Pitman Press).

Walfrod, Geoffrey (ed.) (1987) *Doing Sociology of Education* (Philadelphia: Palmer Press).

West, C., [D. H. Zimmerman] (1987) 'Doing Gender', *Gender and Society*, vol. 1, no. 2, pp. 125–151.

Winder, Bayly (1965) *Saudi Arabia in The Nineteenth Century* (New York: St. Martin's Press).

Youssef, Nadia (1976) Women in Development: 'Urban Life and Labor', in Irene Tinker (ed.), *Women and World Development* (New York: Overseas Development Council).

Youssef, Nadia (1976b) 'Women in the Muslim World', in Lynne Ightizin and Ruth Ross (eds), *Women in The World: A Comparative Study* (Santa Barbara, Cal.: Clio Books).

Youssef, Nadia (1977) 'Education and the Upsurge of Female Modernism in the Muslim World', *Journal of International Affairs*, vol. 30, no. 2.

Bibliography

United Nations Publications

United Nations (1984) *Improving Concepts and Methods For Statistics and Indicators on the Situation of Women* (New York).

United Nations (1985) *Report on the World Social Situation* (New York).

United Nations (1989) *Compendium of Statistics and Indicators on the Situation of Women – 1986–*, (Department of International Economic and Social Affairs, Statistical Office, New York).

Unesco (1970) *The Education and Advancement of Women* (Paris).

Unesco (1984) *Social Science Research and Women in the Arab World* (London: Dover).

Unesco (1985) *Female Participation in Higher Education. Enrollment Trends: 1975–82* (Division of Statistics, Paris, February).

Unesco (1988a) *Education Statistics – Latest Year Available* (Paris, January).

Unesco (1988b) *Compendium of Statistics on Illiteracy (30). Statistical Reports and Studies* (Division of Statistics on Education. Office of Statistics, Paris).

Other Unesco statistics: Run Date 11 April 1989 (Paris).

Kingdom of Saudi Arabia: Official Publications

Ministry of Justice (1974) *Conferences on Muslim Doctrine and Human Rights in Islam* (Riyadh).

Ministry of Planning (1985–90) *The Fourth Year Development Plan (1985–90)* (Riyadh).

Ministry of Planning (1990–5) *The Fifth Year Development Plan 1990–95* (Riyadh).

Ministry of Information (1989) *Saudi Arabia: Education and Human Resources (Riyadh).*

Ministry of Education (1974) *Statistical Summaries on the Kingdom of Saudi Arabia.*

Ministry of Education (1975–6) *Statistical Summaries on Education in Saudi Arabia* (Center for Statistical Data and Educational Documentation).

Ministry of Education (1977–8) *Statistical Summaries on Education* (Center for Statistical Data).

Ministry of Education (1979–80) *Preliminary Summary Statistics on Education in The Kingdom of Saudi Arabia.*

Ministry of Education (1980–1) *Summary Statistics on Higher Education in Saudi Arabia* (Directorate General for Development of Higher Education).

Ministry of Education (1985) *Education and Human Resources Information.*

Ministry of Education (1988–9) *Statistical Summary – The General Presidency of Girl's Education.*

Arabic-Language Sources

Note: these are in Arabic alphabetical order
Publications

Al-Abrashi, Muhammad Atiyya: **Makanat al-Mar'a fi-l-Islam**
Matba'at al-Sha'ab, Cairo, 1971

Ibrahim, Hasan Ali: **Nisa lahunna fi-t-Ta'rikh al-Islami Nasib**
Maktabat al-Nahdha al-Masriyya, Cairo, 1963

Ibrahim, Sayyid Muhammad: **Ta'rikh al-Mamlaka al-Arabiyya as-Su'udiyya**
Riyadh, 1973

Ibrahim, Sayyid Muhammad: **Al-Hayat al-Ijtima'iyya bi-l-Mamlaka al-Arabiyya as-Su'udiyya**
Cairo, 1960

Ibrahim, Abdul Majid: **Al-Mar'a fi-l-Islam**
Cairo, 1976

Ibn Abi Usaibi'a: **Tabaqat al-Atibba'**
Cairo, Bulaq

Ibn Bishr, Uthman ibn Abdullah: **Unwan al-Majd fi Ta'rikh Najd**
Riyadh, 1974

Ibn Taimiyya, Ahmad ibn Abdul Halim: **Hijab al-Mar'a al-Muslima wa Libasuha fi-s-Salat**
Riyadh

Ibn Hajar: **Al-Isaba fi Asma' as-Sahaba**
Cairo, Bulaq

Ibn as-Sanousi, Abu Ridhwan Zaghloul: **Al-Mar'a baina-l-Hijab wa-s-Sufour**
Dar Maktabat al-Hayat, Beirut

Ibn Abdul Wahhab, Muhammad: **Kitab at-Tawhid**
Riyadh

Ibn Kathir: **Tafsir al-Qur'an al-Azim**, 3 volumes
Beirut, 1969

Ibn Manzour, Muhammad ibn Makram: **Lisan al-Arab**, 1–3
Dar Lisan al-Arab, Beirut, 1970

Ibn Hisham, Abdul Malik: **As-Sira an-Nabawiyya**, 1–4
Cairo, 1936

Abu Rida, Muhammad Abdul Hadi: 'Al-Mar'a fi-l-Islam', from the book **Dirasat 'an Awdha' al-Mar'a fi-l-Kuwait wa-l-Khalij**
Women's Socio-Cultural Association, Kuwait, 1975

Abu Shadi, Ahmad Zaki: **Thawrat al-Islam**
Dar Maktabat al-Hayat, Beirut

120   *Bibliography*

General Arab Women's Federation, Office of the Secretariat, Baghdad:
Istratijiyat al-Mar'a al-Arabiyya; al-Khiyar ath-Thalith
Economic and Social Commission for Western Asia (ESCWA), 1990

Abu-l-Ma'ati, Kamal Jawdat: **Wazifat al-Mar'a fi-l-Islam**
Cairo, Dar al-Huda, 1980

Ismail, Muhammad al-Hijri: **Mir'aat al-Mar'a**
Tunis, 1963

Al-Ashqar, Umar Sulaiman: **Al-Mar'a baina Dua'at al-Islam wa
Ad'iyaa at-Taqaddum**
Maktabat al-Falah, Kuwait, 1980

Al-Afghani, Jamal ed-Din. Complete Works, collected by Muhammad
Amara
Dar al-Kitab al-Arabi, Cairo, 1968

Al-Afghani, Said: **Al-Islam wa-l-Mar'a**
Damascus, Matba'at at-Taraqqi, 1945

Al-Afghani, Said: **A'isha wa-s-Siyasa**
Dar al-Fikr, Beirut, 1971

Al-Shaikh, Hasan ibn Abdullah: **Al-Mar'a fi-l-Islam**
(World Symposium for Islamic Youth, 1975)

Al-Albani, Muhammad Nasir ed-Din: **Hijab al-Mar'a al-Muslima
fi-l-Kitab wa-s-Sunna**
Al-Maktab al-Islami, Beirut, 3rd edition

Al-Albani, Wahbi Sulaiman: **Al-Mar'a al-Muslima**
Dar al-Qalam, Damascus, 1975

Amin, Ahmad: **Zu'ama'al-Islah fi-l-Asr al-Hadith**
Dar al-Kitab al-Arabi, Beirut

Amin, Qasim: **Tahrir al-Mar'a**
Cairo, 1970

Amin, Qasim: **Al-Mar'a al-Jadida**
Cairo, 1911

Al-Bar, Muhammad Ali: **'Amaal al-Mar'a fi-l-Mizan**
Ad-Dar as-Su'udiyya li-n-Nashr, Jeddah, 1984

Al-Bukhari, **Sahih al-Bukhari**
Al-Maktaba al-Salafiya, Cairo 1960

Badran, Abu-l-Ainain: **Ahkam az-Ziwaj wa-t-Talaq fi-l-Islam**
Cairo, 1967

Benoist-Méchin: **Abdul Aziz Al-Saud:Sirat Batal wa Mawlid
Mamlaka**: Translated by Abdul Fattah Yaseen
Dar al-Kitab al-Arabi, Beirut, 1965

Al-Bahnasàwi, Salim: **Makan al-Mar'a baina-l-Islam wa-l-Qawanin al-'Alamiyya**
Dar al-Qalam, Kuwait

Al-Bahi, Muhammad: **Al-Islam wa Ittijah al-Mar'a al-Muslima al-Mu'asira**
Dar al-I'tisam, Cairo

Baihum, Muhammad Jamil: **Al-Mar'a fi-t-Tarikh wa-sh-Shara'i'**
Beirut, 1921

Baihum, Muhammad Jamil: **Al-Mar'a fi-l-Islam wa fi-l-Hadhara al-Gharbiyya**
Dar at-Tali'a, Beirut, 1980

Tuffaha, Ahmad Zaki: **Al-Mar'a wa-l-Islam**
Dar al-Kitab al-Lubnani, Beirut, 1979

Al-Tuwaijiri, Hammoud bin Abdullah: **As-Sarim al-Mashour 'ala Ahl at-Tabarruj wa-s-Sufour**
Aleppo. 1974

Thabit, Munira: **Thawra fi-l-Burj al-'Aji**
Mudhakkirati fi Ishrin Am 'an Huquq al-Mar'a as-Siyasiya
Kuwait

Thabit, Nasir: **Al-Mar'a wa-t-Tanmiya wa-t-Taghayyurat al-Ijtima'iyya al-Murafiqa**
Dhat al-Salasil Publications, Kuwait, 1983

Al-Thaqib, Fahd Thaqib: **Al-Mar'a al-Kuwaitiyya wa-l-'Amal**
Kuwait University, 1979

Al-Jahiz: Rasà'il al-Jahiz, collected by Haroun
Cairo, 1979

Gibb, H.A.: **Al-Ittijahat al-Haditha fi-l-Islam**
Beirut, 1961

Al-Jabri, Abdul Muta'ali Muhammad: **Al-Muslima al-'Asriyya**
Dar al-Ansar, Cairo, 1979

Al-Jabri, Abdul Muta'ali Muhammad: **Al-Mar'a fi-t-Tassawur al-Islami**
Maktabat Wahba, Cairo, 1975

Al-Jaziri, Abdul Rahman: **Kitab al-Fiqh 'ala-l-Madhahib al-Arba'a**
Cairo

Jamal, Ahmad Muhammad: **Nisa'una wa Nisa'uhum: Takrim al-Islam li-l-Mar'a**
Taif, Dar Thaqif

Jamal, Ahmad Muhammad: **Makanaki Tuhmadi**
Tihama Publications, Jeddah, 4th edition, 1984

122 *Bibliography*

Al-Jamili, Sayyid: **Ahkam al-Mar'a fi-l-Qur'an**
Dar al-Kitab al-Arabi, Beirut, 1984

Women's Socio-Cultural Association of Kuwait: **Al-Mar'a wa-t-Tanmiya fi-th-Thamaninat,** vols. 1–2, Ashraf Ali, edited and published by Dr. Yahya Faiz al-Haddad
Kuwait University, 1982

Women's Socio-Cultural Association of Kuwait: **Dirasaat 'an Awdha' al-Mar'a fi-l-Khalij wa-l-Kuwait**
Matabi' Mu'assasat Fahd al-Marzouq as-Suhufiyya, Kuwait, 1975

Al-Jandoul, Said Abdul Aziz: **Al-Jins an-Na'im fi Zill al-Islam**
Mu'assasat ar-Risala, Beirut, 1980

Al-Jundi, Anwar: **Harakat Tahrir al-Mar'a fi Miràt al-Islam**
Dar al-Ansar, Cairo

Al-Jundi, Anwar: **Al-Mar'a al-Muslima fi Wajh at-Tahaddiyat**
Dar al-I'tisam, Cairo, 1979

Jawhari, Tantawi: **Tafsir al-Jawahir**
Cairo

Al-Jawhari, Mahmoud Muhammad: **Al-Akhawat al-Muslimat wa Bina' al-Usra**
Dar ad-Da'wa li-t-Tab', Alexandria

Al-Jawhari, Mahmoud Muhammad: **Al-Ukht al-Muslima Asas al-Mujtama' al-Fadhil**
Dar al-Ansar, Cairo

Al-Hamid, Muhammad: **Hukm al-Islam fi Musafahat al-Ajnabiyya**
Zarqa, Jordan, 1981

Al-Hamid, Muhammad: **Nikah al-Mut'a fi-l-Islam**
Hama

Al-Hamid, Muhammad: **Rahmat al-Islam li-n-Nisa**
Dar al-Ansar, Cairo, 3rd edition, 1978

Al-Haddad, Tahir: **Imra'atuna fi-sh-Shari'a wa-l-Mujtama'**
Tunis, Ad-Dar at-Tunusiya li-n-Nashr, 1977

Harb, Muhammad Tala'at: **Tarbiyat al-Mar'a wa-l-Hijab**
Al-Manar Printing House, Cairo, 2nd edition, 1323 A.H.

Hassanein, Muhammad Ahmad: **Al-Jalis al-Anis fi-t-Tahdhir 'amma fi Tahrir al-Mar'a min at-Talbis**
Al-Ma'arif al-Ahliya Printing House, Egypt, 1899

Hussein, Ahmad: **Wa Walid wa ma Walada**
Al-Maktaba al-'Asriya, Beirut, 1975

Al-Husseini, A'isha Ahmad: **I'dad wa Tanmiyat al-Qiyadat al-Idariyya an-Nisa'iyya fi Qita' at-Ta'lim al-'Ali fi-l-Mamlaka al-Arabiyya as-Su'udiyya**
Cairo, 1985

Al-Husseini, A'isha Ahmad: **Al-Mar'a wa-t-Tanmiya fi l-Mamlaka al-Arabiyya as-Su'udiyya**
Women's Socio-Cultural Association, Kuwait, 1981

Al-Hussein, Ahmad Abdul Aziz: **Al-Mar'a wa Makanatuha fi-l-Islam**
Al-Mukhtar al-Islami Printing House, 1981

Hammoud, Hassan: **Mushkilaat al-Mar'a al-Arabiyya fi-t-Ta'lim wa-l-'Amal**
Arab League Educational, Cultural and Scientific Organization, Tunis, 1982

Humeidan, Ahmad: **Al-Mar'a wa-l-Haraka an-Nisa'iyya fi-l-Bahrain**
Dar at-Tali'a, Beirut, 1981

Hanna, George: **Ahadith ma' al-Mar'a al-Arabiyya**
Dar Beirut, Beirut, 1958

Khaki, Ahmad: **Al-Mar'a fi Mukhtalif al-'Usur**
Dar al-Ma'arif, Cairo, 1947

Al-Khatib, Abdul Karim: **Ad-Da'wa al-Wahhabiyya: Muhammad ibn Abdul Wahhab**
Dar ash-Shuruq, Jeddah, 1974

Khalil, Khalil Ahmad: **Al-Mar'a al-Arabiyya wa Qadhaya at-Taghyir**
Dar at-Tali'a, Beirut, 1985

Khamis, Muhammad Atiyya: **Al-Haraka an-Nisa'iyya wa Silatuha bi-l-Isti'mar**
Dar al-Ansar, Cairo

Al-Kholi, al-Bahi: **Al-Islam wa Qadhaya al-Mar'a al-Mu'asira**
Dar al-Qalam, Kuwait, 1984

Al-Kholi, al-Bahi: **Al-Mar'a bain al-Bait wa-l-Mujtama'**
Dar al-Uruba, Cairo, 1965

Khayrat, Ahmad: **Markaz al-Mar'a fi-l-Islam**
Dar al-Ma'arif, Cairo, 2nd edition

Khayyat, Abidiya Ismail: **Dawr at-Ta'lim al-'Ali fi-t-Tanmiya al-Iqtisadiyya wa-l-Ijtima'iyya fi-l-Mamlaka al-Arabiyya as-Su'udiyya**
Dar al-Bayan al-Arabi, Jeddah, 1983

124   *Bibliography*

Darwaza, Muhammad Izzat: **Al-Mar'a fi-l-Qur'an wa-s-Sunna**
Al-Maktaba al-'Asriyya, Saida, 1967

Darwaza, Muhammad Izzat: **'Asr an-Nabi**
Dar al-Yaqza al-Arabiyya, Beirut, 1964

Darwaza, Muhammad Izzat: **Ad-Dustur al-Qur'ani**
Dar Ihya' al-Kutub al-Arabiyya, Aleppo, 1956

Al-Dawalibi, Muhammad Ma'rouf: **Wadh' al-Mar'a fi-l-Islam**
Dar al-Kitab al-Lubnani, Beirut, 1981

Ad-Dailami, Naziha Jawdat: **Namudhaj min Mashakil al-Mar'a al-Arabiyya**
Tunis, 1958

Ar-Razi, al-Fakhr: **At-Tafsir al-Kabir**
Al-Maktaba al-Bahiya, Cairo

Radhi, Ali Abdul Jalil: **Al-Mar'a al-Muslima al-Yawm**
Maktabat al-Anglo-Masriyya, Cairo, 1954

Ar-Rashid, Abdul Aziz: **Ta'rikh al-Kuwait**
Dar Maktabat al-Hayat, Beirut, 1978

Ridà, Muhammad Rashid: **Huquq an-Nisa fi-l-Islam wa Hazzuhunna fi-l-Islah al-Muhammadi al-'Amm**
Beirut, Al-Maktab al-Islami

Ridhwan: **Khatar al-Tabarruj wa-l-Ikhtilat**
Mu'assasat ar-Risala, Beirut, 1974

Az-Zarkali, Khair ed-Din: **Shibh al-Jazira fi 'Ahd al-Malik Abdul Aziz**
Beirut, 1970

Az-Zamakhshari, Mahmoud ibn Umar: **Tafsir al-Kashshaf**, 1–3
Cairo, 1948

Az-Zamili, Mahdiya Shahhada: **Libas al-Mar'a wa Zinatuha fi-l-Fiqh al-Islami**
Dar al-Furqan, Amman, 1983

Zain al-Abidin, Suhaila: **Masirat al-Mar'a as-Su'udiyya ila aina?**
Ad-Dar as-Su'udiyya li-n-Nashr, Jeddah, 1984

Zain al-Abidin, Suhaila: **Al-Mar'a baina-l-Ifrat wa-t-Tafrit**
Ad-Dar as-Su'udiyya li-n-Nashr, Jeddah, 1984

As-Salim, Hidayat Sultan: **Nisa fi-l-Qur'an**
Kuwait Government Printing Press, Kuwait

As-Sadani, Nuriya: **Ta'rikh al-Mar'a al-Kuwaitiyya**, from **Mudhakkirati Khilal Sab'at Ashr 'Am 1963–1980**
Kuwait, vol. 2, 1980, (vol. 1, 1972) published

As-Sudairi, Fahd: **Al-Mamlaka al-Arabiyya as-Su'udiyya 'inda Muftaraq at-Tariq: Al-Tahaddi al-Ijtima'i, al-Wadh' al-Iqtisadi, an-Nizam as-Siyasi**
Beirut, 1970

Su'ad, Ibrahim Salih: **Adhwa' 'ala Nizam al-Usra fi-l-Islam**
Tihama, Jeddah, 1984

Sa'id, Amin: **Sirat al-Imam Muhammad ibn Abdul Wahhab**
Dar al-Malik Abdul Aziz, Riyadh, 1975

As-Sa'id, Sana: **Wujuh wa Qadhaya'**
Kitab al-Yawm, Cairo

Samira, bint al-Jazira al-Arabiyya: **Yaqzat al-Fatat al-Arabiyya as-Su'udiyya**
Al-Maktab at-Tijari, Beirut, 1963

Sharara, Wadhdhah: **Al-Ahl wa-l-Ghanima: Muqawwimaat as-Siyasa fi-l-Mamlaka al-Arabiyya as-Su'udiyya**
Dar at-Tali'a, Beirut, 1981

Ash-Sha'rawi, Muhammad Mutawalli: **Al-Fatawi al-Kubra**
Maktabat at-Turath al-Islami, Cairo, 1987

Shams ed-Din, Muhammad Ja'far: **Al-Islam wa-l-Mar'a fi Haqq Taqrir al-Masir**
Dar at-Ta'awun li-l-Matbu'aat, Beirut

Shalabi, Ra'ouf: **Istawsu bi-n-Nisa Khairan (Nazariyyat al-Islam fi Shu'oun al-Mar'a)**
Isa Al-Babi al-Halabi, Cairo

As-Sabouni, Abdul Rahman: **Mada Hurriyat az-Zawjain fi-t-Talaq fi-sh-Shari'a al-Islamiyya**
Damascus, 1962

Salih, Su'ad Ibrahim: **Adhwa' 'ala Nizam al-Usra fi-l-Islam**
Dar Tihama, Jeddah, 2nd edition, 1984

As-Salih, Subhi: **Al-Mar'a fi-l-Islam**
Al-Mu'assasa al-Arabiyya li-d-Dirasaat wa-n-Nashr, Beirut, 1980

As-Sabbagh, Leila: **Al-Mar'a fi-t-Ta'rikh al-Arabi**
Ministry of Culture and Guidance, Damascus, 1975

As-Simari, Majid: **Az-Ziwaj fi-l-Islam wa Inhiraf al-Muslimin 'anhu**
Beirut, 1979

Dhanawi, Muhammad Ali: **Az-Ziwaj al-Islami amam at-Tahaddiyat**
Al-Maktab al-Islami, 2nd edition, Beirut

At-Tabari, Muhammad ibn Jarir: **Tafsir at-Tabari: Jami' al-Bayan fi Tafsir al-Qur'an**
Cairo, Dar al-Ma'arif

126   *Bibliography*

Zahir, Ahmad Jamal: **Al-Mar'a fi Duwal al-Khalij al-Arabi**, Dirasa Maidaniya
Dhat as-Salasil, Kuwait, 1983

Abdul Baqi, Zaidan: **Al-Mar'a bain ad-Din wa-l-Mujtama'**
An-Nahdha al-Misriyya, Cairo, 1977

Abdul Hamid, Ibrahim Muhammad: **Al-Mar'a fi-l-Islam**
Ad-Dar al-Qawmiyya, Cairo, 1964

Abdur-Rabb, Nawwab ed-Din: **'Amaal al-Mar'a wa Mawqif al-Islam minhu**
Dar al-Wafa li-t-Tiba'a wa-n-Nashr, Mansoura, 1986

Abdur-Rahman, A'isha (bint ash-Shati'): **Nisa' an-Nabi**
Dar al-Ma'arif, Cairo, 1979

Abdul Aziz, Izzat: **Al-Mar'a al-Muslima wa Dawruha fi-l-Mujtama' al-Islami wa-l-Insani**
Dar al-Murjan li-t-Tiba'a, Cairo, 1983

Abdul Fattah, Camelia: **Fi Sikulujiyat al-Mar'a al-'Amila**
Maktabat al-Qahira al-Haditha, Cairo, 1972

Abdul Wasi', Abdul Wahhab Ahmad: **At-Ta'lim fi-l-Mamlaka al-Arabiyya as-Su'udiyya**
Dar al-Kitab al-Arabi, Beirut

Abboud, Abdul Ghani: **Al-Usra al-Muslima wa-l-Usra al-Mu'asira**
Atr, Nur ed-Din: **Madha 'an al-Mar'a**
Dar al-Fikr, Damascus, 1979

Al-Ajlani, Munir: **Ta'rikh al-Bilad al-Arabiyya as-Su'udiyya**, 1-3
Beirut

Al-Udhaimi, Zahir: **As-Su'udiyya wa Tatawwuruha al-Hadith**
Damascus, 1965

Attar, Ahmad Abdul Ghafur: **Saqr al-Jazira** 1-3
Jeddah, 1964

Al-Attar, Abdel Nasser Tawfiq: **Ta'addud az-Zawjat**
Mu'assasat ar-Risala, Beirut

Atawi, Muhsin: **Al-Mar'a fi-t-Tasawwur al-Islami**
Ad-Dar al-Islamiya, Beirut, 1979

Afifi, Abdullah: **Al-Mar'a al-Arabiyya fi Jahiliyyatiha wa Islamiha**
Dar al-Ma'arif, 2nd edition, Cairo, 1932

Afifi, Abdullah: **Al-Mar'a al-Arabiyya fi Zill al-Islam**
Dar al-Kitab al-Arabi, Cairo

Al-Aqqad, Abbas Mahmoud: **Al-Mar'a fi-l-Islam**
Dar al-Hilal, Cairo

Alwan, Abdullah Nasih: **Tarbiyat al-Awlad fi-l-Islam** 1-2
Beirut, 1977

Ammara, Muhammad: **Al-Islam wa-l-Mar'a fi Ra'y Muhammad Abdu**
Al-Mu'assasa al-Arabiyya li-d-Dirasaat, Beirut, 1980

Umaira, Abdul-Rahman: **Nisaa' anzala Allah fihunna Qur'anan**
Riyadh, 1978

Awn, Kamal Ahmad: **Al-Mar'a fi-l-Islam**
Dar al-Ulum, Riyadh, 1983

Uwais, Abdul Halim: **Nizam al-Usra fi-l-Islam**
Ash-Sharika as-Su'udiyya li-l-Abhath, Jeddah, 1985

Ghadiji, Wahbi Sulaiman al-Albani: **Al-Mar'a al-Muslima**
Dar al-Qalam, Damascus, 6th edition, 1984

Al-Gharib, Ramziyya: **At-Tasawwur-ath-Thaqafi wa-l-Ijtima'i li-l-Mar'a fi-l-Bilad al-Arabiyya**
Middle East Research Centre, Ain Shams University

Gharib, Ma'moun: **Nisaa' fi Hayat al-Anbiyaa'**
Maktabat Gharib, Cairo, 1977

Al-Ghadb"n, Munir Muhammad: **Ilaiki ayyatuha-l-Fatat al-Muslima**
Maktabat al-Haramain, Riyadh, 1980

Farisi, Zaki Muhammad Ali: **Ad-Dalil ash-Shamil li-l-Mamlaka al-Arabiyya as-Su'udiyya**
Jeddah, 1990

Fathullah, Hamza: **Bakurat al-Kalam 'ala Huquq an-Nisa fi-l-Islam**
Al-Matba'a al-Amiriya, Egypt, 1308 A.H.

Fakhri, Muhammad: **Tahrir al-Mar'a wa-s-Sufour**
Cairo, Maktabat al-Hilal

Farraj, Izz ed-Din: **Al-Islam wa-l-Usra al-Arabiyya**
Dar al-Fikr al-Arabi, Cairo

Farroukh, Umar: **Al-Usra fi-sh-Shar' al-Islami**
Beirut, 1951

Farfour, Muhammad Salih: **An-Nisa'iyyat min al-Ahadith an-Nabawiyya**
Al-Maktaba al-Haditha, Damascus, 1978

Al-Qurtubi: **Al-Jami' li-Ahkam al-Qur'an** 1–12
Cairo, 1967

Al-Qutb, Ishaq Ya'qoub: **Dawr al-Mar'a fi Zill al-Qiyam wa-t-Taqalid as-Sa'ida fi-l-Mujtama' al-Kuwaiti**
Kuwait University, 1975

Qandil, Buthaina Amin Mursi: **Ittijah al-Fatat al-Muta'allima nahwa 'Amal al-Mar'a**
Maktabat al-Anglo al-Misriyya, Cairo, 1976

Al-Qannouji, Muhammad Sadiq Hasan Khan: **Husn al-Uswa bima thabata 'an Allah wa Rasoulihi fi-n-Niswa**
Mu'assasat ar-Risala, Beirut, 3rd edition, 1976

Kamil, Abdul Aziz: **Ma' ar-Rasoul wa-l-Mujtama'**
Mu'assasat as-Sabah li-n-Nashr, Kuwait, 1980

Kahhala, Umar Rida: **A'laam an-Nisaa' fi 'Alamai al-Arab wa-l-Islam**
Mu'assasat ar-Risala, Beirut, 5th edition, 1984

Kahhala, Umar Ridha: **Al-Mar'a fi-l-Qadim wa-l-Hadith**
Mu'assasat ar-Risala, Beirut, 1983

Kahhala, Umar Ridha: **Az-Ziwaj**
Mu'assasat ar-Risala, Beirut, 1977

Karkar, Ismat al-Din Haram al-Hila: **Al-Mar'a min khilal al-Jami' as-Sahih li-l-Bukhari**
Tunis, Ash-Sharika at-Tunusiyya li-t-Tawzi'

Karkar, Ismat al-Din Haram al-Hila: **Al-Mar'a min khilal al-Ayaat al-Qur'aniyya**
Tunis, Ash-Sharika at-Tunusiyya li-t-Tawzi', 1979

Al-Kirmani, Abdul Qadir Bashir: **Al-Mar'a fi Nazar al-Islam**
Al-Matba'a al-'Ilmiyya, Aleppo, 1928

Mubarak, Ahmad ibn Abdul Aziz: **Al-'Alaqa bain az-Zawjain fi-l-Islam**
Damascus, 1981

Muhammad, Abdul Hamid Ibrahim: **Al-Mar'a fi-l-Islam**
Ad-Dar al-Qawmiyya, Cairo, 1962

Madkour, Muhammad Salam: **Al-Islam wa-l-Usra wa-l-Mujtama'**
Dar an-Nahdha al-Arabiyya, Cairo, 1968

Al-Marsafi, Sa'ad: **Al-'Amal wa-l-'Ummaal bain al-Islam wa-n-Nuzum al-Wadh'iyya al-Mu'asira**

Muslim, al-Imam: **Sahih Muslim**
Cairo, 1928

Al-Mawdoudi, Abu-l-A'la: **Al-Hijab**
Dar al-Fikr, Damascus, 1964

Musa, Nabawiyya: **Al-Mar'a wa-l-'Amal**
Al-Matba'a al-Wataniyya, Alexandria, 1920

An-Ni'ma, Ibrahim: **Al-'Amal wa-l-'Ummaal fi-l-Fikr al-Islami**
Ad-Dar as-Su'udiyya li-n-Nashr, Jeddah, 1985

An-Ni'ma, Ibrahim: **Al-Islam wa Ta'addud az-Zawjaat**
Ad-Dar as-Su'udiyya li-n-Nashr, Jeddah, 1983

Nimr, as-Sayyid Muhammad Ali: **I'dad al-Mar'a al-Muslima**
Ad-Dar as-Su'udiyya li-n-Nashr, Jeddah, 1984

Haikal, Abdut-Tawwab: **Ta'addud az-zawjaat fi-l-Islam wa Hikmat at-Ta'addud fi Azwaj an-Nabi**
Riyadh, 1982

Wafi, Ali Abdul Wahid: **Al-Mar'a fi-l-Islam**
Dar Nahdhat Misr, 2nd edition, Cairo

Wafi, Ali Abdul Wahid: **Al-Musàwat fi-l-Islam**
Dar al-Ma'arif, Cairo, 1962

Watar, Muhammad Tahir: **Makanat al-Mar'a fi-sh-Shu'oun al-Idariyya wa-l-Butulaat al-Qitaliyya**
Mu'assasat ar-Risala, Beirut, 1979

Wajdi, Muhammad Farid: **Al-Mar'a al-Muslima** (reply to Qasim Amin's book **Al-Mar'a al-Jadida**)
Cairo, Matba'a Hindiyya 1912

Official Publications of the Kingdom of Saudi Arabia

General Presidency of Girls' Education
Ta'lim al-Banat fi Sab'at Ashar 'Am 1960-1977
Riyadh, 1977

Department of Girls' Education: Directorate of Girls' Education – Jeddah
Jadwal Ihsa'i 'an al-Bayanat al-Awwaliyya li 'Am 1409 A.H. / 1989

Department of Girls' Education – Jeddah
Masirat Ta'lim al-Banat khilal Rub' Qarn bi Mintaqat Jeddah at-Ta'limiyya (1380-1405 A.H.)
Sharikat al-Madina al-Munawwara li-t-Tiba'a wa-n-Nashr, Jeddah

Department of Girls' Education: **At-Ta'lim fi-l-Mamlaka wa Irtibatuhu bi-l-Khitta al-'Amma li-d-Dawla min khilal Khittat at-Tanmiya ath-Thaniya**
Dar al-Isfahani li-t-Tiba'a, Jeddah, 1399 A.H. / 1979

Ministry of Planning
The Five-Year Development Plan: 1410-1415 A.H. / 1990–1995

King Abdul Aziz University
Nash'a wa Tatawwur Qism at-Talibaat
Sharikat al-Madina al-Munawwara li-t-Tiba'a wa-n-Nashr, Jeddah

King Abdul Aziz University: Female Students' Section
Statistics of the Academic Year 1407 A.H.

Ministry of Higher Education
Tatawwur at-Ta'lim fi-l-Mamlaka al-Arabiyya as-Su'udiyya khilal ashr Sanawaat
1390–1400 A.H. / 1970-1980, Riyadh

Ministry of Education: **Siyasat at-Ta'lim fi-l-Mamlaka al-Arabiyya as-Su'udiyya**
Riyadh, 1390 A.H. / 1970

Ministry of Education: **Statistical Information and Educational Documentation Centre**
Fusul fi Ta'rikh at-Ta'lim bi-l-Mamlaka (Ta'lim al-Banaat)
Riyadh, 1402 A.H. / 1982

Ministry of Education: **Educational Statistics in the Kingdom of Saudi Arabia**
Part 14, 1401–1402 A.H. / 1981–1982

Ministry of Planning: **First Development Plan 1390–1395 A.H. / 1970–1975**

Ministry of Planning: **Second Development Plan 1395–1400 A.H. / 1975–1980**

Ministry of Planning: **Third Development Plan 1400–1405 A.H. / 1980–1985**

Ministry of Planning: **Fourth Development Plan 1405–1410 A.H. / 1985–1990**

Ministry of Planning: **Fifth Development Plan 1410–1415 A.H. / 1990–1995**

Civil Service Commission (Western Region branch – Jeddah)
Annual Report for 1404 A.H.

Ministry of Finance and National Economy:
Civil Service Statistics 1405–1406 A.H.

Publications By Women's Associations and Schools

Dar al-Hanan (Jeddah): Al-Nahdha at-Ta'limiyya li-l-Fatat as-Su'udiyya 1380–1405 A.H. (Jeddah 1405 A.H.)

Women's Charitable Association at Jeddah: The Association's annual report 1408–1409 A.H.

Doctoral and M.A. Theses

Umayya Sulaiman al-Bassam
Dawr al-Mar'a fi Tanmiyat al-Mujtama' al-Mahalli
Dirasa 'an Mintaqat ad-Dir'iya – al-Mamlaka al-Arabiyya as-Su'udiyya
M.A. degree

Alexandria University 1977

Fatima Abdullah al-Khatib
Taghayyur al-Wadh' al-Ijtima'i li-l-Mar'a wa Atharuhu fi Taghyir Dawr az-Zawja dakhil al-Usra as-Su'udiyya
Dirasa Maidaniya 'ala 'Ayyina fi-l-Usar al-Hadhariyya bi Madinat Jeddah
Master's degree in sociology, Cairo 1981

Khawla Ahmad al-Nuri
Mushkilaat al-'Amal fi Riyadh al-Atfal min Wujhat Nazar al-Mudiraat wa-l-Mu'allimaat
Master's degree in education
Baghdad University, Faculty of Education, 1980

Abdullah, Muhammad Abdul Aziz as-Suhail
Tatwir at-Ta'lim fi-l-Jazira al-Arabiyya
D. Litt. degree, Alexandria University

Salwa Ibrahim al-'Ammar
Athar al-Mustawa at-Ta'limi wa-l-Iqtisadi – al-Ijtima'i fi Ittijah Talabat al-Marhalatain al-Jami'iyya wa-th-Thanawiyya Nahwa 'Amal al-Mar'a fi-l-Mamlaka al-Arabiyya as-Su'udiyya
Master's degree, Jordan University, Faculty of Arts, 1982

Muhammad Youssuf al-Hashshash
Dawr al-Jami'aat fi Tanmiyat al-Quwa al-Bashariyya fi-l-Mamlaka al-Arabiyya as-Su'udiyya
Master's degree, King Abdul Aziz University, Faculty of Education at Makkah, 1400 A.H.

Abidiya Khayyat
Dawr at-Ta'lim fi-t-Tanmiya al-Iqtisadiyya wa-l-Ijtima'iyya fi-l-Mamlaka al-Arabiyya as-Su'udiyya
Master's degree, Umm al-Qura University at Makkah, 1401 A.H.

As'ad Umar Azhar
At-Ta'lim ath-Thanawi fi-l-Mamlaka al-Arabiyya as-Su'udiyya wa Dawruhu fi I'dad al-Quwa al-'Amila
Master's degree, King Abdul Aziz University, Faculty of Education at Makkah, 1400 A.H.

Yaseen Salih Youssuf Andarqiri
Tanmiyat al-Quwa al-Bashariyya 'ala Dhaw Siyasat al-Istithmar fi-t-Ta'lim ma'a Dirasa Maidaniyya fi Mujtama' 'Asimat al-Mamlaka al-Arabiyya as-Su'udiyya, Madinat ar-Riyadh
Doctorate, Cairo University, 1390 A.H.

Salih Abdullah Buhul
Dawr at-Ta'lim fi-t-Tanmiya al-Iqtisadiyya wa-l-Ijtima'iyya fi-l-Mamlaka al-Arabiyya as-Su'udiyya 1373–1399 A.H.
Master's degree, King Abdul Aziz University

Hikmat Mutawalli al-Urabi
Al-Mar'a al-Muta'allima fi-l-Mujtama' as-Su'udi: Ta'aththuruha wa Ta'thiruha bi-t-Taghyir al-Ijtima'i wa-t-Tahdith ath-Thaqafi
Master's degree, Ain Shams University, Faculty of Arts, Cairo, 1982

Suhaila Muhsin Muhammad Ali
Dawr al-Mar'a as-Su'udiyya fi-t-Tanmiya fi Dhaw ash-Shari'a al-Islamiyya
Master's degree, Higher Institute for Social Service, Riyadh

Ibtisam Abdul Rahman Halwani

'Amal al-Mar'a as-Su'udiyya wa Mushkilaat 'ala Tariq al-'Ata'
Doctoral thesis submitted to Clairmont University in the USA, 1982
Published by Dar Ukaz li-t-Tiba'a wa-n-Nashr, Jeddah, 1987

A'isha Ahmad Abdur-Rahim al-Husseini
I'dad wa Tanmiyat al-Qiyadaat al-Idariyya an-Nisa'iyya fi Qita' at-Ta'lim al-'Ali bi-l-Mamlaka al-Arabiyya as-Su'udiyya
Doctoral thesis, Al-Azhar University, Cairo, 1985

Fatima Umar Nasif
Huquq al-Mar'a wa Wajibaatuha fi Dhaw al-Kitab wa-s-Sunna
Doctoral thesis supervised by Ahmad Tush
Umm al-Qura University, Makkah, 1983

Articles in Arabic Newspapers and Magazines

Hayat Hazza': Mashakil al-Mar'a al-'Amila
(Ukaz, Nos. 7061/18 October 1985, 7069/26 October 1985)

Fatin Abdullah: Dawr al-Mar'a al-Mansi fi-l-Haraka at-Tijariyya
(Ukaz, No. 5666/28 December 1983)

Abdullah al-Ghamdi: Survey: Min huna tabda' Masirat al-Mar'a
(Ukaz, No. 3295/6 Dhu-l-Hijja 1401 A.H.)

Yara Muhammad: Al-Mar'a wa Dawruha fi Khidmat Khitat at-Tanmiya
(Al-Jazira, No. 4882/9 February 1986)

Princess Hussa bint Salman and Princess Jawhara bint Fahd: Al-Fatat as-Su'udiyya tusahim bi Dawriha fi Ruqiy al-Mujtama'
(Ukaz, No. 7175/9 February 1986)

Muhammad Hussein Zaidan: Al-Mar'a fi Majal al-I'lam
(Ukaz, No. 7175/9 February 1986)

Mervet Khalifa, Buthaina Yamani: Survey: Al-Shabbaat yasrukhna: Anqidhuna min hadha-l-Faragh ar-Raheeb
(Ukaz, No. 7028/15 September 1985)

Sayyid Rajab al-Farouq: Nizam at-Ta'lim wa Mutatallibaat al-'Amala
fi-l-Mamlaka al-Arabiyya as-Su'udiyya
(Dirasaat al-Khalij wa-l-Jazira magazine, No. 33, ninth year, January
1983, Kuwait)

Ahmad al-Fanjari: Hawla-n-Niqab
(Al-Quds newspaper, Kuwait, 10/7/1986)

Abdullah al-Nuwaisir: Al-Fatat as-Su'udiyya wa-l-Faragh
(Ukaz, No. 7254/29 April 1986)

Tawfiq al-Qaseer, Iman al-Khatib: Al-Mar'a al-'Amila fi Nazar ar-Rajul
wa-l-Mar'a
(Ukaz, No. 6862/19 February 1985)

Sawsan Mustafa: Survey on: Al-Mar'a as-Su'udiyya wa 'Udwiyatuha
fi-l-Mujtama', al'Amal fi Hayat al-Mar'a Dharura Ijtima'iyya
(Ar-Riyadh, No. 4284, 13/8/1399 A.H.)

Dr. Abdu al-Yamani: Ma hiya as-Sura al-I'lamiyya al-Islamiyya al-
Matluba min al-Mar'a as-Su'udiyya
(Al-Madina, No. 5477/22 Jumada I 1402 A.H.)

Dallal Aziz Dhiya': La Su'uba fi-t-Tawfiq bain al-'Amal wa
Mutatallibat al-Hayat az-Zawjiyya
(Al-Madina, No. 5477/22 Jumada I 1402 A.H.)

Mudhi al-Zahrani: Survey: Fatayat wa Sayyidaat Tumuhuhunna la
tahudduhu hudud
(Ar-Riyadh, No. 5084, 29/5/1402 A.H.)

A. Sulaiman Kanjari: Rabbat al-Bait an-Najiha tuhayyi' ar-Raha
an-Nafsiyya li Zawjiha wa tuwaffir lahu al-Hudu' ba'da 'Ana
al-'Amal
(Ukaz, No. 6217, 7 June 1983)

Aliya Mashikh: Madha haqqaqat al-Fatat as-Su'udiyya wa ma hiya
Mutatallibaatuha
(Ukaz, No. 7182, 16 February 1986)

Haya al-Mani': Al-Mar'a al-Qari'a aina hiya?
(Ar-Riyadh, No. 7388, 14 September 1989)

Sara ar-Rashidan: Mashakil al-Mar'a wa-l-I'lam
(Ar-Riyadh, No. 7378, 4 September 1988)

Ahmad Abdul Qadir Ma'bi: Al-Ikhtilat Adhraruhu wa Asbabuhu
(Al-Madina al-Munawwara, No. 4935, 3 Sha'ban 1400 A.H.)

Adnan Said Ahmad Hassanein: Da'a'im al-Mu'ashara az-Zawjiyya
fi-l-Islam
(Al-Madina al-Munawwara, 17 Sha'ban 1400 A.H.)

134   *Bibliography*

Badriyya al-Bishr: Al-Mar'a as-Su'udiyya. 'Amala yumkin an yustaghna
biha 'an al-'Amala al-Ajnabiyya ar-Rijaliyya fi majalaat 'idda
(Ar-Riyadh, No. 6508, 8 April 1986)

Maqboul al-Juhani: Al-Mar'a la taqill 'an ar-Rajul fi-l-Majal al-'Ilmi
(Al-Madina al-Munawwara, No. 4448, 27 Dhu-l-Hijja 1398 A.H.)

Khuzaima al-Attas: Amjad Rida, Muna Murad: Tahqiq 'an Mustaqbal
al-Khirrijaat fi Nazar Ustadhaat al-Jami'a
(Ukaz, No. 8620, 18 February 1990)

Ali Abboud Ahmad Ma'di: Dawr al-Mar'a fi-l-Bina
(Ad-Da'wa magazine, No. 709, 22 Sha'ban 1393 A.H.)

Nura ar-Rifa'i: Dharurat Itahat Fursat at-Tadrib li-l-Mar'a al-'Amila
Ahdaf Markaz Tadrib al-Fatayaat 'ala-t-Tafsil wa-l-Khiyata
(Ukaz, No. 7259, 4 May 1986)

Nadia as-Sa'idi: Khirrijaat al-Khidma al-Ijtima'iyya
(Ar-Riyadh, No. 8387, 13 September 1988)

Abdullah al-Mushidd, Head of the Legal Advisory Committee at Al-
Azhar: Decision on birth control for health reasons
(Sayyidati magazine, No. 439, 13/8/1989)

Ali at-Tantawi: Hikm Sitr Wajh al-Maraa'
(Sayyidati Magazine, No. 440, 20/8/1989)

Sayyid al-Darsh: 'Amal al-Mar'a kharij Baitiha
(Al-Sharq al-Awsat newspaper, 13, 14 and 15/4/1986)

Ahmad Shalabi: 'Amal al-Mar'a
(Al-Watan newspaper, 29 May 1986)

Nadia as-Sa'idi: Sayyidaatuna fi-l-Kharij
(Ar-Riyadh, No. 7342, 30 July 1988)

Hussa al-Tammami: In'idam al-Wa'y as-Sihhi li-l-Mar'a wa
Mushkilaatuha
(Ar-Riyadh, No. 7367, 24 August 1988)

Sa'wadat kaafat al-Waza'if an-Nisa'iyya
(Ukaz, No. 8064, 6 August 1988)

Salahuddin AlMunajjed: Ra'y fi Tahrim Hukm al-Mar'a
(Al-Hayat, No. 9761, Saturday-Sunday 2-3 September 1989)

Amjad Mahmoud Ridha: Al-Jami'a tahtafi bi-t-Talibaat al-Mutakharrijaat
(Ukaz, No. 8617, 14/1/1989)

Sihr Husam ed-Din al-Umawi: Al-Ihtimam bi-l-Mar'a al-'Amila as-
Su'udiyya
(Al-Madina al-Munawwara, No. 4971, 15 Ramadhan 1400 A.H.)

Suhair al-Subki: At-Tifl wa-l-Mar'a wa Uslub at-Tarbiya fi Dawra Tadribiyya li Raf' Mustawa al-Mar'a al-'Amila fi Majal al-Umuma wa-t-Tufula
(Ar-Riyadh, No. 5074, 18/5/1402 A.H.)

Gulf Affairs Editor: Al-Mar'a al-Khalijiyya wa-l-'Amal
(Ar-Riyadh, No. 6250, 3 August 1985)

Sabah ad-Daoud: Hiwar ma'a Sayyidaat hawla 'Amal al-Mar'a: Ahdafuhu, Mu'awwiqaatuhu wa-l-Arbah wa-l-Khasa'ir
(Ar-Riyadh, No. 4641, 18/11/1400 A.H.)

Director of Girls' Education at Al-Ahsa: Hadaf Ta'lim al-Banaat huwa at-Tathqif wa laisa at-Tawzif
(Al-Jazira, No. 3101, 10 February 1981)

Abdul Wahid al-Humayyid: 'Uzlat al-Jami'a .. am 'Uzlat al-Mujtama'
(Ukaz, No. 8694, 13 March 1990)

Ahmad Shawqi al-Fanjari: Al-Mar'a al-Muslima wa Haqq al-'Amal as-Siyasi wa-t-Tashri'i
(Al-Hayat, No. 9942, 31 March-April 1990)

Maarouf ad-Dawalibi: Dawr al-Mar'a fi-l-Mujtama' al-Islami
(Al-Sharq al-Awsat, No. 4129, 19/3/1990)

Sana' Arab: Al-Kulliyaat la tastaw'ib kull ar-Raghibaat fi-d-Dirasaat al-'Ulya
(Ukaz, No. 8107, 18/9/1988)

Tayyiba al-Idrisi: Khirrijaat ath-Thanawiyya al-'Amma
Nasma' 'an al-Waza'if ash-Shaghira, wa 'ind at-Taqaddum nusaab bi Khaibat Amal idha lam tatawaffar al-Waza'if, falimadha la tuftah Ma'ahid Fanniyya li-n-Nisa. Madha yaf'al Diwan al-Khidma al-Madaniyya amam Alaaf al-Khirrijaat?
(Ukaz)

Sara ar-Rashidan: Mustaqbal at-Ta'lim yahtaj ila Taqwim
(Ar-Riyadh, No. 7386, 12 September 1988)

Haya al-Mani': Saif al-Banaat bila Kitab
(Ar-Riyadh, No. 7352, 9 August 1988)

Sara ar-Rashidan: Manahij Ta'lim al-Mar'a hal ma zalat muwakiba laha
(Ar-Riyadh, No. 7357, 14 August 1988)

Haya al-Mani': Fi Mas'alat al-Qubul al-Jami'i 85% na'am wal-Baqi la
(Ar-Riyadh, No. 7374, 31 August 1988)

Hussa at-Tammami: Li-l-Atfal Hidhanaat Masa'iyya, hal najiduha?
(Ar-Riyadh, No. 7354, 11 August 1988)

Thurayya Muhammad Ahmad: Khirrijaat at-Tafsil wa-l-Khiyata yatasa'alna: Ma masirunba'dat-Takharruj? Mata tusbih al-Mashagil Nisa'iyya? Nurid Khitat Madrusa li Tawzif al-Khirrijaat
(Ar-Riyadh, No. 7346, 3 August 1988)

Lu'lu'a Buqshan: Khirrijaat al-Jami'aat wa-l-Kulliya ... Hal at-Tafriqa Manhajiyya am Wazifiyya?
(Ar-Riyadh, No. 7346, 3 August 1988)

Siham Ka'ki: Min al-Jam'iyaat an-Nisa'iyya: Al-Mar'a tahtaj hadhihi-d-Dawraat li-t-Taw'iya as-Sihhiyya
(Ar-Riyadh, No. 7389, 15 September 1988)

Nadia as-Sa'idi: 'An al-Bi'a: Wa-l-Mar'a tahtaj at-Taw'iya aydhan
(Ar-Riyadh, No. 7363, 20 August 1988)

Hussa at-Tammami: Qubul Khirrijaat ath-Thanawi kaifa nuqanninuhu
(Ar-Riyadh, 18 August 1988)

Ahmad Bahjat: Tajriba Najiha li Sayyidat A'mal Su'udiyya
(Interview, Sayyidati magazine, No. 459, 31/12/1989)

Badi'a Hasan: 'Alam adh-Dhahab wa Asraruhu
(Interview, Ukaz newspaper, No. 6968, 17 July 1985)

Mervet Khalifa: Al-Islam wa Hurriyat al-Mar'a
(Ukaz, No. 6968, 17 July 1985)

Nadia as-Sa'idi: Fi-s-Sina'a li-l-Mar'a Dawr Qadim
(Ar-Riyadh, No. 7370, 27 August 1988)

Samia al-Ammouri: 'Ajeeb .. Ghareeb .. ma ra'aytu
(Ukaz, 20 August 1988)

Hussa at-Tammami: Limadha tubkhas Huquq hadhihi-l-Waza'if?
(Ar-Riyadh, No. 7375, 1 September 1988)

Lu'lu'a al-Ghamdi: Ayyuhuma awwalan: At-Ta'lim am az-Zawaj?
(Ukaz, No. 8570, 30 December 1989)

Sara ar-Rashidan: Marakiz al-Buhuth 'an al-Mar'a man yatabannaha
(Ar-Riyadh, 29 August 1988)

Ahmad Muhammad Jamal: Ma tuqbal fihi Shahadat al-Mar'a wa ma la tuqbal
(Al-Sharq al-Awsat, 11/6/1986)

Ahmad Muhammad Jamal: Ma tuqbal fihi Shahadat al-Mar'a wahdaha
(Al-Sharq al-Awsat 11/7/1986)

Sada Amr Jalalat al-Malik bi Ta'min ad-Dirasaat al-'Ulya li-l-Banaat fi-d-Dakhil
(Ar-Riyadh, 6 August 1985, 20 Dhu-l-Qa'ada 1405 A.H.)

Dawr Bariz li-l-Mar'a al-Khalijiyya
(Ar-Riyadh, No. 514, 17 April 1982)

Al-Mar'a fi-l-Khalij tadkhul kull Majalaat al-'Amal
(Al-Anwar, No. 7053, 10/8/1980)

Second Regional Conference on Women in the Gulf and the Arabian
Peninsula
'Qadhiyat al-Mar'a Mushkila Ijtima'iyya yusharik fi halliha al-Jinsan
ma'an'
(Sayyidati magazine, vol. 1, No. 8, 1981)

Al-Mar'a as-Su'udiyya 'Amala yumkin an yustaghna biha 'an al-'Amala
al-Ajnabiyya ar-Rijaliyya fi Majalaat 'idda
(Ar-Riyadh, 18 April 1986)

Jami'aatuna as-Su'udiyya hal addat Dawruha
(Ar-Riyadh, No. 4471, 5/4/1400 A.H.)

Hadith Shamil 'an at-Taliba al-Jami'iyya as-Su'udiyya: Ijabiyaatuha wa
Salbiyaatuha
(Al-Madina al-Munawwara, No. 5428, 2 Rabi II 1402 A.H.)

Hussa at-Tammami: Mahw al-Ummiya
(Ar-Riyadh, No. 7385, 30 Muharram 1409 A.H.)

Fatawa' al-Shaikh ibn Baz
(Al-Madina, No. 6621, 1 Ramadhan 1405 A.H.)

Abdul Aziz ibn Baz: Fatawa 'an al-Mar'a fi-l-Islam
(Al-Mujtama' magazine, Kuwait, 24/4/1979)

Ra'y al-Malik Fahd fi-l-Mar'a wa-l-'Amal
(Ukaz, No. 7722, 25 August 1987)

Al-Mar'a wa-l-'Amal
(Ar-Riyadh, No. 4632, 1980)

Sa'wadat Waza'if at-Ta'lim
(Ukaz, No. 8617, 14 February 1990)

Al-Mar'a as-Su'udiyya wa-l-'Amal fi-l-Qita' al-Khass
(Ukaz, No. 8570, 30 December 1989)

Mushkilat al-Faragh 'ind al-Fatat as-Su'udiyya
(Ukaz, 20 August 1988)

Al-Mu'allima as-Su'udiyya Kathirat al-Ghiyab
(Ukaz, No. 7192, 26 February 1986)

As-Su'udiyaat kaifa yusharikna fi-t-Tanmiya ath-Thaqafiyya
(Ukaz, No. 6952, 1 July 1985)

Tatawwur at-Ta'lim al-'Ali fi-l-Mamlaka khilal Ashr Sanawaat
(Al-Madina al-Munawwara, No. 5526, 12 Rajab 1402 A.H. / 1982)

Ta'lim al-Banaat wa-l-Ibti'ath
(Ar-Riyadh, No. 4584, 29/8/1400 A.H.)

286 Milyun Riyal li Insha' Majma' li Ta'lim al-Banaat bi Makkah
(Ar-Riyadh, No. 4502, 21/5/1400 A.H.)

7 Su'udiyaat yatasallamna Shahadaat at-Takharruj min Kulliyat at-Tibb
bi Lahore
(Al-Madina al-Munawwara, No. 4835, 3 Rabi II 1400 A.H.)

Awamir Samiya bi Man' Dirasat al-Banaat bi-d-Duwal al-Ajnabiyya
(Ukaz, No. 6283, 12 Dhu-l-Qa'ada 1403 A.H. / 20 August 1983)

Dalil Bayan al-Khidma al-Madaniyya (Directorate-General of Planning
and Manpower – Ahsa Directorate): for the years 1403, 1404, 1405,
1406, 1407, 1408 and 1409 A.H.

Al-Bunuk an-Nisa'iyya
(Ar-Riyadh, No. 5026, 16/1/1982, and At-Tijara magazine No. 293,
Rabi II 1405 A.H.)

Al-Mar'a as-Su'udiyya ta'mal fi-l-I'lam wa-t-Tibb
(Al-Fajr newspaper (United Arab Emirates), No. 808, 12/7/1980)

Tahrir al-Mar'a fi Nitaq ash-Shari'a al-Islamiyya
(Ar-Ra'ida magazine, May 1978, p. 8, No. BUC 4)

'Amal al-Mar'a fi-l-Mizan
(Ukaz, No. 6271, 8 August 1983)

Al-Mar'a as-Su'udiyya bain al-Bait wa-l-Wazifa
(Al-Madina al-Munawwara, No. 4935, 2 Sha'ban 1400 A.H.)

Ma'a Awwal Tabibaat Su'udiyaat yatakharrajna min Jami'at ar-Riyadh
(Ar-Riyadh, No. 4548, 17/7/1400 A.H.)

Salbiyaat wa Ijabiyaat al-Mar'a al-'Amila fi Mujtama'ina
(Ar-Riyadh, No. 4455, 25/3/1400 A.H. / 1980)

Fatayaatuna bain al-'Amal wa-z-Zawaj wa-d-Dirasaat al-'Ulya
(Ar-Riyadh, No. 4482, 28/4/1400 A.H. / 1980)

Al-Mar'a as-Su'udiyya Sayyidat A'mal
Elle (Oriental) magazine, No. 136, November 1985)

Al-Fatat as-Su'udiyya wa-l-Faragh: Abdullah an-Nuwaisir
(Ukaz, No. 7254, 29 April 1986)

Al-Mar'a fi Hayat Imam ad-Da'wa Muhammad ibn Abdul Wahhab
(Ar-Riyadh, 8/3/1980)

Aina Andiyat al-Fatayaat
(Ar-Riyadh, No. 5090, 31/3/1982)

Rasmiyya Ali Khalil: Al-Mar'a wa-t-Tanmiya ma'a Ishara ila-l-Khitta al-Khamsiyya ath-Thaniya li-l-Mamlaka al-Arabiyya as-Su'udiyya
(Al-Iqtisad wa-l-Idara magazine, King Abdul Aziz University, No. 8, Muharram 1399 A.H./December 1978, Ukaz edition)

Muhammad Hussein Zaidan: Al-Mar'a fi Majal al-I'lam
(Ukaz, No. 7175, 9 February 1986)

Nadia Hijab: Himayat al-Mustaqbal: Al-Mar'a wa-t-Tanmiya al-Mutawasila
(Al-Sharq al-Awsat newspaper, No. 3971, 12/10/1989, p. 9)

Thurayya Ubaid ash-Sharif: Al-Mar'a al-Arabiyya tataqaddam ila aina?
(Qadhaya al-Mar'a, 8 March 1981, pp. 4–5)

Suhair Lutfi: Ru'yat al-Mar'a fi-l-Fikr al-Islami al-Mu'asir
(Al-Yaqza al-Arabiyya magazine, year 1, March 1985, pp. 93–112)

Dallal al-Khalidi: Al-Jins an-Na'im fi Zill al-Islam
(Al-Jazira, No. 6968, 29 Muharram 1401 A.H. / 7 December 1980)

Mervet Khalifa: Al-Islam wa Hurriyat al-Mar'a
(Ukaz, No. 6968, 17 July 1985)

Muhammad Hassan al-Rifi: Muqawwimaat al-'Amal fi-l-Islam
(Al-Sharq al-Awsat, 16/4/1986, p. 10)

Sayyid al-Darsh: 'Amal al-Mar'a kharij Baitiha
(Al-Sharq al-Awsat, Sunday 13/4/1986, p. 14, Monday 14/4/1986, p. 10, and Tuesday 15/4/1986, p. 10)

Amina as-Sa'id: Al-Mar'a al-Arabiyya wa Tahaddi al-Mujtama'
(An-Nadwa al-Lubnaniyya 1967, vols. 11–12)

Shaikh Hassan Khalid: Al-Mar'a fi 'Urf al-Islam
(Al-Fikr al-Islami magazine, Beirut, year 6, May 1975)

Shaikh Hamza Shukr: Makanat al-Mar'a fi-l-Islam wa-l-Adyan
(Al-Fikr al-Islami magazine, year 6. No. 5, May 1975)

Shaikh Mutawalli al-Sha'rawi: Mawqif al-Islam min al-Mar'a
(Ukaz, 26 Rajab 1399 A.H., p. 7)

Abdul Muhsin ad-Daoud: Al-Islam rafa'a Makanat al-Mar'a wa a'taha Huquqaha fi-l-A'mal wa-z-Zawaj
(Ar-Riyadh, No. 4423, p. 6, 17/2/1400 A.H.)

Adnan Sa'id Ahmad Hassanein: Da'a'im al-Mu'ashara az-Zawjiyya fi-l-Islam
(An-Nadwa, 17 Sha'ban 1400 A.H., p. 3)

Abdul Mu'min Muhammad Nu'man: Huquq al-Mar'a
(Al-Madina al-Munawwara, No. 4991, 13 Shawwal 1400 A.H., p. 7)

Iman al-Khatib: Al-Mar'a al-'Amila fi Nazar ar-Rajul wa-l-Mar'a
(Ukaz, No. 6826, 19 February 1985)

Fatima Mandili: Ma hiya as-Sura al-I'lamiyya al-Islamiyya al-Matluba
min al-Mar'a as-Su'udiyya?
(Al-Madina al-Munawwara, No. 5477, 1982)

Abdullah Nasih Alwan: Al-Mar'a wa-l-'Amal fi-l-Islam
(Al-Madina al-Munawwara, No. 6815, 24 Rabi I 1406 A.H., p. 11)

Abdul Baqi Atallah: Al-Mar'a fi-l-Islam
(Ukaz, No. 6366, 7 Safar 1404 A.H. / 11 November 1983)

Habiba al-Burqadi: Afaaq al-'Amal al-Ijtima'i al-Arabi wa Dawr al-
Mar'a fihi
(Shu'oun Arabiyya magazine, 31 September 1983)

Khidhr Zakariya: Mulahazaat hawla Waqi' al-Mar'a al-Arabiyya wa
Dawruha fi-t-Tanmiya
(Shu'oun Arabiyya magazine, 31 September 1983)

Abdullah an-Nuwaisir: Al-Fatat as-Su'udiyya wa-l-Faragh
(Ukaz, No. 7254, 29 April 1986)

Salih al-Zir: Al-Mar'a la taqill 'an ar-Rajul fi-l-Majal al'Ilmi
(Al-Madina al-Munawwara, 27 Dhu-l-Hijja 1398 A.H., No. 4448)

Tawfiq Ahmad Su'ud al-Qasir: Al-Mar'a al-'Amila fi Nazar ar-Rajul
wa-l-Mar'a
(Ukaz, No. 6826, 19 February 1985)

Badriyya al-Bishr: Al-Wazifa an-Nisa'iyya ash-Shaghira
(Ar-Riyadh, 29 March 1986, No. 6488)

Abdullah Kanun: Al-Islam wa-l-Mar'a
(Da'wat al-Haqq magazine, Morocco, vol. 20, 5 May 1979, pp. 4–11)

Nafisa Ibrahim Naji: Shakhsiyat al-Mar'a fi-l-Qur'an al-Karim
(Al-Madina al-Munawwara, No. 5505, 20 Jumada II 1402 A.H.)

Shaikh Ahmad ibn Abdul Aziz Al-Mubarak: Al-Mar'a fi-l-Islam
(Al-Yawm newspaper, No. 3202, 2 Dhu-l-Hijja 1401 A.H.)

Aliya Muhammad al-Khayyat: Al-Musawa fi-l-Islam
(Al-Bilad, 20 Jumada II 1399 A.H., No. 6138)

Ahmad Abdul Qadir Mu'in: Al-Ikhtilat Adhraruhu wa Asbabuhu
(Al-Madina al-Munawwara, No. 4935, 2 Sha'ban 1400 A.H.)

Wajiha Muhammad Sabah: Dawr al-Mar'a al-Muslima fi-l-Qadim wa-l-
Hadith
(Al-Jazira, 4 April 1981, No. 3154)

Safa Muhammad Rifa'at: Kaifa ahsana ilaina al-Islam wa a'la Qadrana Ma'shar an-Nisa
(An-Nadwa newspaper, 27 Safar 1400 A.H.)

Abdul Aziz ibn Rashid: Ma yuthar hawl al-Mar'a
(Ad-Da'wa magazine, No. 706, Sha'ban 1399 A.H.)

Fatima Mandili: Al-Mar'a as-Su'udiyya wa 'Udhwiyatuha fi-l-Mujtama'
(Member of An-Nahdha an-Nisa'iyya Association at Riyadh, summarized in Ar-Riyadh newspaper, No. 4284, 13/8/1399 A.H.)

Index of the Qura'nic Verses

Index of the Hadith Al Nabawi (Sayings of the Prophet Muhammad)

145

'The zina of the eye is the look; the zina of the hand is the touch; the zina of the tongue is the word; the zina of the feet is to walk following our desires, and the zina of the mouth is the kiss.' 55

Index of Subjects

Index of Personal Names

Index of Places